SHERMAN

★ THE | GENERALS ★

SHERMAN

The Ruthless Victor

★ THE | GENERALS ★

Agostino Von Hassell and Ed Breslin

THOMAS NELSON
Since 1798

NASHVILLE   DALLAS   MEXICO CITY   RIO DE JANEIRO

Published in Nashville, Tennessee, by Thomas Nelson. Thomas Nelson is a registered trademark of Thomas Nelson, Inc.

Thomas Nelson, Inc., titles may be purchased in bulk for educational, business, fund-raising, or sales promotional use. For information, please e-mail SpecialMarkets@ThomasNelson.com.

Library of Congress Cataloging-in-Publication Data

Von Hassell, Agostino.

Sherman : the ruthless victor / Agostino Von Hassell and Ed Breslin.

p. cm. -- (The generals)

Includes bibliographical references.

ISBN 978-1-59555-133-7

1. Sherman, William T. (William Tecumseh), 1820-1891. 2. Generals--United States--Biography. 3. United States. Army--Biography. 4. United States--History--Civil War, 1861-1865--Campaigns. I. Breslin, Ed. II. Title.

E467.1.S55V66 2011

355.0092--dc23

[B]

2011027231

Printed in the United States of America

11 12 13 14 15 WOR 6 5 4 3 2 1

Contents

A Note from the Editor

TO CONTEMPLATE THE lives of America's generals is to behold both the best of us as a nation and the lesser angels of human nature, to bask in genius and to be repulsed by arrogance and folly. It is these dichotomies that have defined the widely differing attitudes toward the "man on horseback," which have alternatively shaped the eras of our national memory. We have had our seasons of hagiography, in which our commanders can do no wrong and in which they are presented to the young, in particular, as unerring examples of nobility and manhood. We have had our revisionist seasons, in which all power corrupts—military power in particular—and in which the general is a reviled symbol of societal ills.

Fortunately, we have matured. We have left our adolescence

with its gushing extremes and have come to a more temperate view. Now, we are capable as a nation of celebrating Washington's gifts to us while admitting that he was not always a gifted tactician in the field. We can honor Patton's battlefield genius and decry the deformities of soul that diminished him. We can learn both from MacArthur at Inchon and from MacArthur at Wake Island.

We can also move beyond the mythologies of film and leaden textbook to know the vital humanity and the agonizing conflicts, to find a literary experience of war that puts the smell of boot leather and canvas in the nostrils and both the horror and the glory of battle in the heart. This will endear our nation's generals to us and help us learn the lessons they have to teach. Of this we are in desperate need, for they offer lessons of manhood in an age of androgyny, of courage in an age of terror, of prescience in an age of myopia, and of self-mastery in an age of sloth. To know their story and their meaning, then, is the goal here and in the hope that we will emerge from the experience a more learned, perhaps more gallant, and, certainly, more grateful people.

Stephen Mansfield

Series Editor, *The Generals*

Introduction

GENERAL WILLIAM TECUMSEH Sherman led a controversial and contradictory life. He undoubtedly fought with superior skill and strategy toward the preservation of the Union, but, like his Confederate adversaries, he was proslavery. Many historians consider him a military genius whose superior strategy, tactics, and logistics spared the lives of many of his troops; but he simultaneously granted them free rein to wreak havoc upon innocent civilians. His troops' crimes ranged from theft and destruction of personal property to rapes and beatings and, in some horrendous instances, murder. One of Sherman's signature actions as he tore through Georgia on his famous "March to the Sea" was the torching of civilian homes, often stately mansions or attractive farmhouses, rarely of any military or strategic value. Burning down cotton gins and mills was justifiable during the Civil War in that the South sold cotton in exchange for arms. Burning homes and barns was not. Sherman's treatment of civilians amounted to nothing short of a crime against humanity. For such actions, Sherman is considered the principal originator of what he called "hard war," and what the world ever since has called "total war." His signature quote that "war is hell" is emblematic of his role as principal originator. But in this dubious enterprise Sherman is not alone. Grant, Sheridan, and Lincoln are also frequently charged as fellow originators. Of course the slaughter of the innocents in the Bible that gave rise to the Jewish holiday of thanksgiving known as Passover would qualify as a type of total warfare, but what is meant by the modern phrase is the wanton use indiscriminately of weapons of major destruction against civilian populations, which first found wide and systemized use in the American Civil War courtesy of its four originators.

Grant and Lincoln were more distant from the unnecessary brutality visited on the "enemy" directly by Sherman. But Sheridan, leader of the marauding Union cavalry that vandalized the Shenandoah Valley, shares Sherman's reputation for inflicting unnecessary pain and suffering upon the enemy—soldiers and noncombatants alike. Both men believed such excessive pain and suffering were more effective than any strategic or tactical objective. Their rationale is what we would today call "psychological warfare"—warfare designed to convince the opposition to surrender rather than suffer any further casualties. Grant, Sherman's mentor, modeled the tenets of *invasive* warfare, which involved advancing his forces deep into enemy territory, out of reach of a secure supply line, and living off the land. Grant did that at Vicksburg and came out the victor. Grant, however, limited his destruction to targets having military value: rail lines, train stations and depots, cotton gins, and other businesses and buildings that could aid his opponent in the war. Grant effectively destroyed or impeded the functional capacity of his opponent while leaving citizens and noncombatants for the most part unmolested. He placed a governor on his military engine. Sherman did not. He defined the enemy as anyone residing below the Mason-Dixon Line who might possibly disagree with his personal political views, especially regarding secession and states' right, and who might therefore sympathize with the aims and aspirations of the Confederacy—an entity he abhorred. Anyone branded as such Sherman considered a "traitor." Whatever destruction and pain such traitors suffered, however horrific, was deserved. Sherman was an absolutist. The world and all the issues in it were black or white. There were no shadings, no extenuating circumstances.

Despite the debate over states' rights having been the central issue of his young republic from its inception, Sherman saw no reason for this difference of opinion to rise up once again, eight decades after it first formed the basis of debate at the Constitutional Convention in Philadelphia. The punishment for this rebellion had to be severe.

As extreme as Sherman's behavior was, there may have been a psychological deformity at the root of his extreme behavior. As most of his biographers point out, mental illness had a long history in his family, especially on his mother's Hoyt side. Not only did this reoccur in Sherman, but also in his son, Tom, a Jesuit

priest who inherited his father's eloquence and dictatorial disposition but became so inflamed that he often had to be restrained
by his Jesuit superiors for rash and incendiary statements. And
like several of his Hoyt forebears, Tom eventually spent time in
an asylum.

Sherman addressed his own mental illness in a rare instance
of humility and self-awareness when he famously remarked, while
speaking of Grant: "He stood by me when I was crazy and I stood
by him when he was drunk, and now, sir, we stand by each other
always." Many of Sherman's comments regarding the legendary
general weren't as chummy, however, despite Grant's repeated
sacrifices and white lies on Sherman's behalf. Grant endured
Sherman's criticism after the war, when Grant was president and
Sherman served as his general-in-chief. Sherman spurned Grant
as softhearted and softheaded in his handling of "the Indian
problem," bluntly stating that "extermination" was the appropriate and expedient solution to the unfortunate presence of Native
Americans in their own land.

An unashamed white supremacist, Sherman also faulted
Grant for his concern over the fair and just treatment of ex-
slaves. On the record he proclaimed the "inferiority" of blacks
and viewed Grant again as overly compassionate in this regard.
Though the racist Sherman served as a Union general in the Civil
War, moral concern on the issue of slavery was not a factor for him.

His brutality was not limited to blacks and Native Americans.
At the onset of the war, Sherman was convinced the Confederate
forces, though initially better organized and trained, would eventually prove to be no match for the Union army; yet he would end

up wiping out an unthinkable number of civilian lives and home-steads. He did so knowing full well they were utterly defenseless and despite his proclaimed love for the South, often stated in his letters, written when he was a young officer stationed there nearly two decades prior to the outbreak of the Civil War.

Directly after Atlanta fell to him, Sherman stooped to destruc-tion and pillage, unleashing his soldiers on defenseless civilians, many of them women and children. Even considering the psy-chological strategy of total war, these actions were inexcusable: the South had lost the ability to mount any defense, let alone carry forward a good fight. Sherman himself had predicted the South's demise with absolute certainty five years earlier in Louisiana. Many historians claim that Sherman, on his March to the Sea and then to Raleigh, operated at "great risk" in "enemy territory," but this may overstate the case. Sherman and his army marched nearly seven hundred miles from Atlanta to Raleigh. They numbered sixty thousand strong. They incurred *six hun-dred* fatalities—1 percent of 1 percent. This is hardly evidence of fierce fighting. Sherman and his army, though technically in enemy territory, encountered no real resistance.

Meanwhile, in Virginia, Grant and Lee were each suffering fatalities in five, not three, figures. In the waning weeks of the war, Grant refused to allow Sherman to rush his army north from Raleigh, close in on Lee, and crush him. Grant knew that his great and gifted opponent was defeated. Sherman, nevertheless, wanted in on the kill, and sulked when Grant countermanded his wish and ordered him to stay put in North Carolina. Sherman's character pales starkly in comparison to that of his friend and leader, General Grant. The deft manner in which Grant handled all aspects of Lee's surrender is a matter of historical record. At the conclusion of the meeting, Grant famously removed his hat when Lee mounted his horse Traveller to ride away into history. All of the Union staff officers present in the Appomattox courtyard promptly removed their hats too. An expressionless Lee, aristocratic dignity intact, tipped his hat to Grant, flicked the reins, and rode off. For the five years left to him on earth, Lee would abide no negative comment about Grant in his presence. When President Andrew Johnson, Lincoln's successor, informed Grant that he intended to charge Lee with treason and prosecute him accordingly, Grant promised to resign on the spot the minute any charges were filed. In no manner was Lee to be harmed or dishonored. Johnson relented. Sherman's character seems just the opposite of these two great generals. He was self-serving, even in victory. Eager to ingratiate himself with the Southern upper classes after the war, Sherman offered overly generous terms to Johnston at his surrender in North Carolina, exceeding the parameters Lincoln had set. Grant was forced to rush to Bennett Place, Sherman's headquarters outside Durham, to rectify the matter.

Sherman could also be disingenuous. He expressed contempt for journalists, as well as for politicians and lawyers. He tried to have Thomas Knox of the *New York Herald* court-martialed and executed for espionage. But this did not prevent Sherman from using the power of the press, even courting and manipulating it, for his own purposes. In fact, conscious of controlling his image and his place in history, Sherman was in many ways before his time.

Though still professing to loathe the press, postwar he

manipulated it well and combined it effectively with his less-than-truthful memoirs to present himself in a favorable light. Sherman most likely held his breath when word reached him that Grant's memoirs were soon to be published. He probably feared that Grant would contradict him by setting the record straight. Ever gracious, Grant feathered his way around Sherman's self-glorifying revisions.

Perhaps the most distasteful, even shameful, episode of hypocrisy was Sherman's public distancing from his wartime commands. He disavowed responsibility for his troops' actions on the march through Georgia and the Carolinas, though only a disingenuous man could pretend that his often wayward troops would have followed his specific but totally unrealistic orders, such as the injunction to avoid profanity while commandeering the property of Southern civilians.

What made Sherman so vicious and vindictive? Perhaps he agreed with his wife on a certain point. For example, in a letter discussing the overgenerous terms of surrender he had offered Johnston—the terms Grant had to correct and revoke—Ellen Sherman blamed the Confederacy for the death of their oldest son: "However much I differ from you I honor and respect you for the heart that could prompt such terms to men who have cost us individually one keen great pang which death will alone assuage—the loss of Willy."

In fact, Willy died of a combination of camp dysentery and typhoid fever when visiting his father on the battlefield in Mississippi after the siege of Vicksburg, but of course, a parent's grief often is not comforted by logic.

No man is one-dimensional, and for all his faults Sherman had a softer side. He could be personable, even affectionate—as he was to his students in Louisiana, who often perceived him as friendly and outgoing. He was brilliant, as well. In fact, his ability to absorb vast amounts of detail facilitated all of his career choices, not just those having to do with the military. Despite these outstanding attributes, history remembers him as a brutal warrior, and this overshadows all evidence of a kinder, more gifted man.

Whatever motivated Sherman to such senseless retribution—whether innate family insanity; the childhood traumas resulting from the early death of his father and the resulting separation from his mother and his grandmother; the death of his son on Southern soil; or perhaps, an inherent, inexhaustible capacity for pure malice—the result was catastrophic for the country. Mark Twain remarked that the Civil War "uprooted institutions that were centuries old . . . transformed the social life of half the country, and wrought so profoundly upon the entire national character that the influence cannot be measured short of two or three generations." He was wrong. The bitterness of the South has lasted down to this day, seven or eight generations later.

Reading accounts of the war in Sherman's letters and memoirs, one recalls Stephen Dedalus's remark in James Joyce's novel *Ulysses*: "History is a nightmare from which I am trying to awake." But we cannot awake from history. Far better it is, then, to look it in the face and to learn from its glory and its depravity. Both are abundantly evident in the life of William Tecumseh Sherman.

ONE

Named for a Warrior

GENERAL WILLIAM TECUMSEH Sherman's name didn't include "William" until his Catholic foster mother insisted that he be given a proper Christian name at a formal baptism and added William. No matter—for his whole life, family called him "Cumpy" or "Cump," and later his classmates and fellow officers called him simply "Sherman." There is a story behind "Tecumseh," the unusual original first name. His father, Judge Charles R. Sherman, chose the name because he admired the Shawnee chief who had fought so well for the British during the War of 1812. Chief Tecumseh had presented a deadly threat to the settlers in Ohio when Sherman's forebears first settled there. It was provocative of Charles to name his son after an enemy, and fellow settlers did not appreciate it. When one of them protested, Judge

Sherman replied flatly that "Tecumseh was a great warrior"—and that settled that. This decisive attitude more accurately foreshadows General Ulysses S. Grant's treatment of General Robert E. Lee than General Sherman's inconsistent stance during and after the Civil War. The Shermans were a prominent family of lawyers, judges, militia leaders, and legislators. There had been Shermans in New England since the beginning of the seventeenth century, and the family could trace its roots even further back to the town of Dedham in Essex county, England. Almost certainly the surname "Sherman" derives from "shearman," which indicates the family was involved in the wool trade.

The Shermans quickly distinguished themselves as leaders and professionals in the American colonies. Daniel Sherman sat in the Connecticut General Assembly for three decades and played a fiery role in rallying forces during the American Revolution. Roger Sherman was a member of the "Committee of Five" that wrote the Declaration of Independence in a fetid room above a tavern on Chestnut Street in Philadelphia during the summer of 1776. In 1811, twenty-three-year-old Charles R. Sherman relocated on the advice of his attorney father, Taylor Sherman, to what was then called the "West." He advised Charles to settle down, establish his law practice, raise his family, and seek his fortune. When Charles Sherman took his father's advice and traveled west to Lancaster, Ohio, he fell into a social set made up of the newly booming settlement's principal families. He tactfully positioned himself for judicial assignments and his law practice soon became prosperous. After a short time he became a circuit judge, and then President James Madison appointed him revenue collector for the Third District of Ohio. His father had held this same position in Connecticut. Charles was seeking to relive his father's success, but, being an ambitious man, he overextended his time and his means.

In 1817, the U. S. Treasury Department suddenly declared that it would accept payment only in coin or in U. S. Bank notes. In Ohio, notes drawn on local banks had long been acceptable as loan payments by individuals and were even accepted by the federal government in payment for taxes. Suddenly these notes were worthless as federal payment. Left with significant debt, Charles Sherman was nearly bankrupted by this new law. He pledged to make good on every penny of the debt he had incurred, and this commitment, though admirable, proved onerous in the end. By 1828, he was a circuit judge and a revenue collector, the father of eleven children, struggling with debt, and overloaded with duties and responsibilities.

In time he was offered an appointment to the Ohio Supreme Court but vacillated about taking the position. Finally, he decided to take the job but did not hold it long. After the sudden onset of a fever one year later in 1829, the judge died.

Nine-year-old Tecumseh's world fell apart. This moment would mark the beginning of a new life for the entire family and a season of torturous turmoil for Tecumseh. In many historians' eyes, this serves as the most defining experience in General Sherman's developing psychology.

Friends and family rallied to the widow Mary's side, but it was clear that the family had to be broken up, the children separated. The two oldest had more or less reached adulthood.

Charles Hoyt Sherman was on the brink of graduating from nearby Ohio University in Athens and went to work soon after in an established lawyer's office. His younger sister Elizabeth was already set to marry William Reese. As for the three youngest children, their mother was determined to keep them with her in the family's clapboard house on Main Street. The six middle children, including Tecumseh, were to be dispersed among relatives and friends.

In addition to losing his father and any close contact with his mother, Tecumseh was also separated from his grandmother, Elizabeth Stoddard Sherman, who had earlier migrated west to live with her son Charles and his family, but had to find other living arrangements after Charles died. A strong and sensible woman, Grandmother Stoddard had been a stabilizing influence on the entire family. Now, along with both of his parents, her positive force was gone for young Tecumseh too. It is difficult to say with certainty whether these changes were directly related to the violent frustration of his later years. Undoubtedly, though, these monumental shifts in his home life at such a young age left a permanent mark.

In the eighteen years that Judge Sherman and his wife, Mary, had lived in Lancaster, they had become close friends with the leading families in town, all of whom, like them, lived on Main Street. Charles Sherman made friends with a fellow barrister named Thomas Ewing. Thomas, a year his junior, was not only a genius in the law but also possessed a keen business mind, especially for real estate investment. He prospered, too, as part-owner of the Kanawha Salt Works.

In 1831, Tom was elected to one of the inaugural senate seats for Ohio. Ewing's wife, Maria Boyle, was devoutly Catholic. This was the household young Tecumseh was raised in, and the Ewing influence molded Sherman to a remarkable degree. His new foster mother immediately insisted that a priest baptize young Tecumseh, who carried the name "William Tecumseh" from then on.

Sherman never took his Catholicism seriously, nor any other form of religion. His biological father was a nominal Congregationalist whose strongest affiliation was to the Masons—so much so that on his deathbed he refused to see any member of the clergy and requested a funeral in the Masonic rite. His foster father, Tom Ewing, even more tellingly, never practiced any religion and seems to have regarded all religion as void of meaning. In these matters, Sherman followed in the footsteps of both men his entire life. Sherman lived with the four Ewing children and three other foster children. Maria was a notoriously harsh disciplinarian, unlike her husband. A generous man, Tom insisted that Sherman make himself at home and consider himself equal with Ewing's own children. As any child psychologist can confirm, this transposition rarely works out smoothly and often leaves scars. This seems to have been the case with Sherman.

Tom noted that Sherman was bashful and not fully at home with them. Many years later he commented that he had never known a boy as young as Sherman to be so dutiful and prompt about fulfilling chores and errands. Overly conscientious children often feel deprived of any real childhood.

Nevertheless Sherman was privileged in many ways while growing up. Maria Ewing encouraged all the children to read and insisted they receive a first-class education. Both Judge Sherman and Tom Ewing had been driving forces in setting up the first school in Lancaster, and Sherman attended there with the rest of his foster siblings. When Sherman was twelve years old, the school came under the supervision of an esteemed set of teachers known as the Howe brothers, who then taught all the lessons. From these two gifted instructors, Sherman learned French, Latin, and the rudiments of Greek. He also acquired his first taste of Shakespeare and of Sir Walter Scott, as well as reading a wide range of fiction, history, arithmetic, and geography.

The Ewing household was lavish in contrast to the Sherman home from which William had been removed. Not only did he feel the gnawing insecurity of being an outsider in his new home— of having lost his sense of belonging—he also was aware of the contrast between his wildly successful foster father and his miserably failed natural father. For the remainder of his life, William Sherman refused to discuss the judge, claiming his memories were sparse and sketchy. Furthermore, it seems that living under a legend such as Tom Ewing caused a mixture of admiration and rebellion in Sherman and an inclination to free himself of dependency on his foster father. This proved to be much more difficult than he might have imagined.

Ewing's politics played an undeniable role in Sherman's development. In the senate, Ewing was a staunch Whig and had no time for abolitionists. Sherman permanently adopted both his foster father's political party and his attitude toward slavery, including a sympathy toward the South. Senator Ewing became a ranking member within the Whig Party and hobnobbed with fellow senators Daniel Webster, Henry Clay, and the fiery John C. Calhoun. All three were among the most influential and eloquent senators ever to sit in the upper chamber of Congress. For the most part, Ewing shared a negative view toward President Andrew Jackson with most Whigs, referring to the swashbuckling hero of the Battle of New Orleans as "King Andrew" and deeming his administration tyrannical and hideously corrupt. Ewing and Calhoun parted company over the issue of states' rights, however. Like the late Judge Sherman, Ewing was a bedrock constitutionalist and a devout believer in the importance of the union's preservation. His family considered the union sacred.

So it was that William Tecumseh Sherman acquired his political convictions. At the heart of his civic worldview was a belief in the sanctity of the American union. When the time came in 1861, Sherman was ready and willing to do his part.

Sherman image from LSU—Sherman served as Superintendent at the Louisiana Military Seminary from 1859 to 1861. This painting by Samuel Lockett circa 1860 shows Sherman standing by a window with the school's main building in the background.

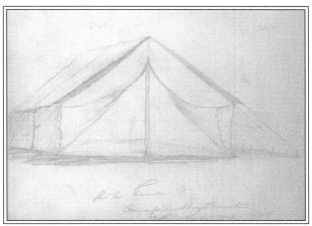

Sketch of a tent in camp near Vicksburg, Mississippi, by William Tecumseh Sherman dated 1863.

Sherman on horseback in Atlanta in 1864.

T W O

At Home at West Point

IN THE SUMMER of 1835, Sherman completed his studies at the Howe brothers' academy. When it came time to choose a career for him, the Ewings followed Charles and Mary Sherman's wishes that Sherman pursue national service in the military. Judge Sherman had wished his third-born son to enter either the army or the navy, but his wife believed the navy too dangerous, and her fears regarding her son's safety took priority. Thus, West Point became the sole option.

Charles Ewing's influence played a primary role in Sherman's appointment to West Point. In 1835 Ewing wrote to Secretary of War Lewis Cass about the possibility of William being admitted. Cass wrote back that the deadline for consideration for that year had passed, but Ewing, persistent and efficient as always, wrote again in early 1836. In short order young Sherman received his appointment to the academy for the class of 1840, admitted as cadets in the fall of 1836. Sherman resigned himself to his fate, initially nervous at the prospect of living under a strict military regimen for four long years. Sherman had some time to kill before he left the following summer for West Point. Again, the senator stepped in. Ever a man with projects under way, Ewing was president of the company in charge of building the Lancaster Lateral Canal, which would connect the town of Lancaster to the larger Ohio Canal. Thanks to him, Sherman acquired a job working as an assistant to the surveyor engaged in laying out the canal path.

This was Sherman's first job, and it paid him half a dollar a day. Like any teenager he enjoyed having his own money, but that was not the job's only benefit. He acquired surveying skills that would prove helpful in his West Point engineering classes. The job also instilled in him a keen awareness of terrain and its possibilities—a critical skill for military command. Yet psychologically there was a dark side to all this good fortune for Sherman. He was developing an aversion to the feeling of indebtedness brought on by his foster father's power and generosity. He had ended up under the senator's roof as a child because of chance, but Sherman's progress in adult life was now beginning to owe itself entirely to Ewing's influence. Sherman struggled for decades to wrest his identity from that connection and pursue goals absent any boost from Ewing. According to his biographers, Sherman, like many intensely driven young men, wanted to emerge as his own man. It's a measure of his commitment to that goal that during the time he worked on the Lancaster Canal he devoted his free time to studying mathematics and French, two core subjects at West Point. In May 1836, the day of departure arrived. Both foster parents and Mary, Sherman's mother, tearfully bid the boy farewell. It was time for the future general to embark on his first long journey. He climbed aboard the waiting stagecoach and headed east for the first time in his life, taking the initial step toward becoming the celebrated conqueror of the Confederacy twenty-nine years later.

Young William was absorbed by his first trip across the country to visit the fabled sites long described by his foster father. At that time in America, the earliest railroads were only one or two years old, and passengers were exposed to smoke and cinders thrown back by prototype engines. It was not uncommon for the clothing of passengers to catch fire. In some instances, the engines—which were merely primitive boilers—had been known to explode and scald passengers.

And so, perhaps wisely, Sherman chose to take a coach instead of a train for the entire trip to Washington. The first three days of travel landed him in Frederick, Maryland, after having been confined the whole trip to the inside of the coach by extremely inclement weather. At Frederick, he exchanged coaches and headed for the capital, avoiding a train ride not only for safety reasons but because he wanted to see the countryside. The love of topography that would make him a fine engineer and military leader already drew him. This last leg of the journey took the remainder of the month of May and on June 1 Sherman showed up in Washington, D.C. at "Mrs. Hill's," the boarding house favored by many senators and where Tom Ewing resided.

Sherman's first taste of Washington must have been overwhelming. At that time Washington was nothing like the sophisticated cosmopolitan metropolis it is today. In fact, it was scarcely more than a giant village with dirt streets that produced clouds of choking dust in the dry season and a mire of mud when the rains came. It was built on swampland, and the city was like a steaming cauldron in the summer months, making the congressional recess a blessed institution very early on.

When Sherman arrived, the capital was anything but placid. President Andrew Jackson, also known as "Old Hickory" and the "hero of the Battle of New Orleans," was stirring things up, revamping the national banking and currency systems and causing dramatic change in many areas. Some suspected Jackson enjoyed stirring up the old wags of the Whig Party, of which Senator Ewing was a prominent and longstanding member. Jackson's fondness for drink and habitual cronyism also drew much criticism, and caricatures of him set a standard for future political cartoonists. In short, Washington was a town in full foment. The impressionable young Sherman went out for a walk one day and, passing the White House, spotted the president pacing the gravel drive, wrapped in his overcoat and cap, looking very much the old soldier and apparently deep in contemplation. The impression the legendary hero made on Sherman was that Jackson was somehow smaller and less monumental than expected. Nevertheless, Sherman watched the president for a full hour from the far side of a wooden fence.

It wasn't long before Sherman was rubbing elbows with some considerably powerful men. On Sherman's first visit to

Washington, Tom Ewing introduced him to—and in some instances had him accompany to political functions—such political luminaries as Henry Clay; John C. Calhoun; Vice President Martin Van Buren, who would later ascend to the presidency; and Daniel Webster. Sherman also became acquainted with former secretary of the navy S. L. Southard, who counseled the cadet-to-be that industry and obedience were the two keys to succeeding at West Point.

Finally, after this whirlwind week, Sherman left for the Hudson River Valley, bound for West Point. Sherman decided to chance the railroad this time and departed from the original B&O station. He made his way north to New York City and took the ferry to Brooklyn to spend short visits with his mother's brothers Charles and James I. Hoyt. A few of the Hoyt family members remembered young Sherman as a wild specimen from "the far West," as Ohio was considered at that time. During this New York City visit, Sherman experienced his first taste of what would become a lifelong passion when he attended a play at the Park Theatre. Sherman would eventually evolve into quite an artistic personality—not only growing in passion for the theater but also developing his writing skills to an admirable extent and becoming an accomplished illustrator through classes at West Point.

When the visits ended, he departed by steamer up the mighty Hudson to the wharf at West Point. The vessel was filled with other excited young men about to be sworn in as cadets. By then, it was the middle of June, and the scenery on the trip up the Hudson from Manhattan was spectacular. The wide blue river, the looming bluffs, the ample foliage of the season, and the wide-open sky composed a magnificent landscape that had inspired many paintings and poems by nineteenth-century American artists. Sherman's impressions on this excursion would ever live in his memory.

The steamer chugged into the wharf at the river's majestic bend, West Point, and Sherman and his future classmates stepped off the gangplank to find themselves on the riverfront beneath the fabled plains. The sixteen-year-old Sherman couldn't have known that he was going to be more at home here than at any other place since his father had died seven years earlier. Here the young man destined for big things would find his métier and would experience a sense of belonging that would resonate for the rest of his life. For now, during this prelude to his turbulent future, he was on terra firma.

When Sherman arrived in 1836, the academy was a mere thirty-four years old. There were only a few buildings, and they were crude structures of wood and stone. There were two barracks, north and south, both primitive. The south barracks was even colder than the north barracks. Neither was comfortable in winter, as the only heat came from small fireplaces. These conditions were largely the result of suspicions of West Point's purpose in the minds of the Washington, D.C. elite. Anything under federal control was deemed questionable and funding suffered from these attitudes. Some legislators questioned whether America needed a national military academy at all.

The national military academy had been haphazard and

disorganized for the first fifteen years of its existence until Colonel Sylvanus Thayer, "the father of West Point," became superintendent in 1817. A valedictorian graduate of Dartmouth in 1807, Thayer was appointed to the academy by President Thomas Jefferson and graduated as a second lieutenant in 1808 after studying there for one year. Nine years later, after service in the War of 1812, Thayer received notice from President James Madison that he was to take over the academy as superintendent. He revamped the school and saved it from dissolution by its legislative critics.

In between Thayer's cadet year and his return as superintendent, the army had posted him to Europe, where he studied mathematics and engineering at the French Institute Polytechnique. He became a brilliant engineer and established West Point as the first bona fide engineering school in America and the prototype for future engineering schools, all of which adopted the West Point texts. Thayer resigned in 1833 after a dispute with a cantankerous Andrew Jackson. By the time Sherman graduated from the academy, it had improved beyond the Thayer years through the leadership of Major Richard Delafield, who took over in 1838. Sherman liked Delafield, nicknamed "Dicky the Punster" for his sarcasm, and their friendship lasted after Sherman's graduation from the school.

Sherman was quickly inducted into West Point. With his solid schooling, thanks to the Howe brothers, he easily passed the basic tests in the three R's. The entrance exam at the time was simple, due to Congress's insistence that West Point remain accessible to the average youth and not be limited to the upper class, already privileged enough to have access to private academies.

Under Delafield, the academy was stocked with a strict, learned faculty who taught a challenging curriculum. A cadet's day was tightly scheduled. There was an onerous demerit system that Sherman violated routinely, causing his overall class standing to be reduced upon graduation to sixth from fourth among forty-two cadets. This downgrade had no bearing on Sherman's overall experience at West Point, which to him was most impressive and pleasing.

The menu at West Point was notoriously bland and consisted mostly of cheap carbohydrates with very little meat, the result of the guidelines of the catering contractor. He considered meat unnecessary in the diet of young healthy men and far too expensive. In response to this culinary regime, Sherman became quite famous at the academy as a "hasher." This meant he was skilled at concocting impromptu snacks, usually late at night, heated over a grill on the fireplace in a remote dorm. The food was usually smuggled from the mess hall or, even better, was sometimes purchased from Benny Haven's, a favorite off-limits tavern and food store within walking distance of the campus. Sherman famously sneaked a bushel of oysters onto the grounds from Haven's and threw a cooking party late one night in the barracks. Because of this and many other habits—such as dressing less strictly than the code called for, showing up late for drill and for reveille, and talking in formation—Sherman received a high number of demerits. There were not as many, however, as he later recalled in his writings. All were born of good spirits rather than a bad nature, though, and he was without a doubt popular with his fellow cadets during his time at West Point. Sherman had no trouble academically, given his solid education and polished upbringing, complemented by his innate intelligence. In fact, he could have ranked even higher in his class, but his interests were diverse and certainly didn't include studying more than necessary.

Though the academy curriculum was weighted heavily for engineering, there were also classes in English grammar. These, combined with his studies in prose back in Lancaster, fashioned within Sherman an extraordinary talent. In fact, both he and a cadet named Sam, a big, somewhat uncouth youth from Ohio who entered West Point when Sherman was a senior, would turn out to be excellent writers and two of the most heavily read memoirists of nineteenth-century America. Sam is famous in history as Ulysses S. Grant.

In terms of military strategy, Sherman learned much from professor Dennis Hart Mahan, an Irish immigrant who had graduated at the top of his West Point class in 1824. Mahan taught the tenets of the great Baron Antoine Henri Jomini, including an emphasis in waging war on the French word *celerite*. Throughout the Civil War, Sherman often focused on *celerite*—the equivalent in English is "swiftness, quickness, or adroitness." Indeed, Sherman was destined to demonstrate *celerite* in warfare and be famously and infamously remembered for it.

Besides the teachings of Professor Mahan, the pervasiveness of Southern culture and values throughout the academy was another dominant influence on Sherman. Southerners had a born-to-lead disposition, reflected in the history of the young country to that point. The South had produced more important national leaders, including presidents, vice presidents, senators, diplomats, and cabinet secretaries, than any other region of the country.

At West Point, this Southern aura of class entitlement took precedence over the Northern traits of democratic equality and the striving middle-class—or, worse, immigrant—emphasis on upward mobility. While the Southerners were polished cavaliers, the Northerners were crude cannoneers. There was a noticeable divide between the gracious planter class and the bustling industrial crowd. In Sherman's class of 1840, and in the classes shortly before and shortly after his, there would be many cadets who later squared off against one another in the Civil War.

In his plebe year—*plebe* is short for *plebian* and is what first-year cadets are derogatorily called at West Point—the seniors on campus included Braxton Bragg, Jubal A. Early, Joseph "Butcher Joe" Hooker, John C. Pemberton, and John Sedgwick. There were such other notables as P. G. T. Beauregard, Irvin McDowell, William J. Hardee, Henry W. Halleck, and Edward O. C. Ord. Alongside Sherman as plebes were George H. Thomas and Stewart Van Vliet. As Sherman moved along for the next three years toward graduation, many prominent names entered in the classes behind his: Don Carlos Buell, Daniel H. Hill, Nathaniel Lyon, John F. Reynolds, Josiah Gorgas, William S. Rosencrans, James Longstreet, Earl Van Dorn, and John Pope. Many of these names echo down to the present not only in historical narrative, but also in the naming of forts and other military installations. Sherman's name would be attached to the workhorse tank used by the U. S. Army in World War II and in Korea.

Not all cadets became soldiers, however. Two classes behind

Sherman at West Point was George Deshon, who, despite a distinguished record as a cadet, would forsake his promising military career and become a Paulist priest. He participated in Sherman's funeral service fifty years later at the request of Sherman's Catholic family. Many other cadets of that era would also pursue careers as clergymen. This trend nettled some critics of the academy, who viewed such religious "defections" as a dangerous development that actually squandered taxpayer funds. To equate the training of America's clergy to "squandering" is questionable, of course. Moreover, by becoming clergymen these religious cadets were only doing what often came naturally to educated young men in those days, when Harvard, Yale, and Princeton—all of which began as seminaries—produced thousands of clergymen from their outstanding divinity programs.

At West Point, Sherman found a family structure that suited him more naturally than the Ewing family, where he had never resolved his feelings of alienation and indebtedness. He was well liked, so much so that he never warranted excessive discipline. In fact, by earning so many demerits he managed to injure his class standing on his own quite well enough. When he disrupted the classes of Thomas Hart Mahan with chatter or with joshing, the great professor found Sherman's affability too charming to counter harshly.

His classmates long commented on Sherman's outstanding honesty and integrity. He was a man who valued honor and rectitude within any organization. West Point's order reassured him, vanquishing the great displacement and uncertainty he had felt in the wake of his father's untimely death. It gave him the sense of belonging he craved. Unfortunately, it could not resolve the conflicts and contradictions inflicted by his childhood. These would torment and haunt him his entire life. Based on his later years, when he rarely spent time at home with his wife and children, it seems reasonable to conclude that he never resolved the internal conflict that resulted from his attraction to and revulsion from scenes of domestic happiness, from which he had felt excluded at the Ewing household.

The South, unfortunately, presented such scenes in abundance. This prevalent and blissful state of domesticity seems to have ignited in Sherman a gratuitous pyromania, justified within himself as an exigency of war. All of this lay in the future, though. After graduation from West Point, Sherman was attached to the artillery and dispatched to the South.

THREE

The Enchanting South

IN MID-OCTOBER 1840, the Third Artillery was in Florida, engaged in what is now called the Second Seminole War. The First Seminole War was the result of the actions of then major general Andrew Jackson, who in 1818 attacked and brutally punished the Seminole people living in Florida for harboring runaway slaves. It was President Andrew Jackson who had precipitated this second "war" with the Seminoles. The Seminoles had refused to accept his proposed banishment to lands west of the Mississippi in Arkansas and in response had launched their attacks on U. S. Army forts in Georgia and Florida.

Second Lieutenant Sherman was sent to the steamy swamps of Florida for his first military assignment. Before he left the North, however, Sherman had to play Sherman one last time. After spending his post-graduation furlough in Lancaster, Ohio, he violated regulations when he entered a West Point barracks, which officers were forbidden to do unless authorized. Superintendent Delafield duly reprimanded Sherman, issuing a condemnatory letter about him for this action. Perhaps because of Sherman's heartfelt letter of apology to the superintendent, the secretary of war dismissed this transgression as a minor infraction and took no action. The letter of apology also preserved Sherman's friendship with Delafield, a mentor to him. This friendship would prove helpful through the years. As Sherman sailed out of New York Harbor, he was likely contemplating the new dynamic developing between his foster sister Ellen and him. While he was at West Point, she had been his chief correspondent and confidante, aside from his brother John Sherman. On this latest visit in Lancaster, Sherman's relationship with Ellen had shown signs of evolving from foster sibling to suitor. If Sherman had intended to separate his fate from the influence of Tom Ewing, he was on the wrong path. In due time, he married Ewing's daughter.

Ellen was at this time still a student at the Academy of the Visitation in Washington, D.C., which Sherman sarcastically referred to as her "nunnery." This seemingly lighthearted joke symbolized what became William and Ellen's strongest disagreement—Sherman's aversion to organized religion. It would always present an obstacle for Ellen, who in matters of faith took after her mother. The other lifelong thorn in their relationship was Sherman's profession. Ellen adopted a skeptical view of military life and its hardships: the geographic distance it would put between William and his family and its low pay in comparison to other professions and commercial ventures. When the twenty-year-old Sherman sailed south that autumn, such marital friction lay in the future. As a young man enjoying his first taste of official life, he was focused instead on reporting to his new post. There he joined his West Point chums George H. Thomas and Stewart van Vliet. All three were posted to the Third Artillery, which had been fighting the Seminoles in Florida's swamps and everglades for the last three years, mostly without success.

In Washington, William Henry Harrison's death in 1841 turned the political world upside down. The aftermath did not deal a winning hand for Tom Ewing.

The summer before, while Sherman was developing feelings for Ellen at home in Lancaster, Ewing had been hard at work on the campaign trail for Harrison, the Whig candidate and celebrated war hero of Tippecanoe. Emulating Andrew Jackson's successful image as a war hero, Ewing and the Whigs pitched Harrison as a frontiersman, despite their deep-seated loathing for "Old Hickory." When the Democrats insulted Harrison by satirizing him as a rustic fool cloistered in his cabin quaffing hard cider, their strategy backfired. Harrison won.

Harrison appointed Ewing as secretary of the treasury, but this and all the rest of the Whigs' plans went up in smoke when Harrison died of pneumonia a month after taking office. John Tyler, his vice president, succeeded him and to the chagrin of the Whigs instituted a Democratic agenda. Senator Tom Ewing's tenure as secretary of the treasury was over. He resigned and protested the policies implemented by President Tyler, particularly his failure to reestablish the National Bank of the United States, which had been dissolved by President Jackson.

William Tecumseh Sherman was far away from these conflicts. He was glad to be entering his military career with its high ethical standards, and in doing so to be removed from his family. The ordered life of an officer shielded him from both his natural and his foster families' lives of lawyering and politics. As Sherman continued to do all of his life, he viewed such political shenanigans as hopelessly shabby and sordid. These views created in Sherman a wary view of democracy, an attitude that only deepened into ironclad conviction with age.

When Sherman reached the bar of the Indian River in Florida for the first time, he transferred to a whaling boat rowed by four men and directed by a guide. After cresting the mouth of the Indian River, he changed yet again, this time to an even smaller boat, again rowed by the four men. They took him two miles up a channel between the Mangrove Islands until they debouched into a wide lagoon in front of Fort Pierce. Here Sherman joined Company A, Third Artillery Regiment, a unit actively engaged in the war to displace the Seminoles, and assumed his duties as a second lieutenant.

Sherman's first taste of war as an officer was disillusioning. It bore no resemblance to the lessons taught by Dennis Hart Mahan at West Point. Though the enemy was constant, they were not fixed in battle positions. The Seminoles were waging guerrilla warfare, a legacy Native Americans originated and perfected before teaching it by painful example to colonial Americans, who in turn used it wisely and well against the British Empire. For any soldier trained in conventional warfare, converting to guerrilla warfare can be extremely frustrating. Sherman was no exception.

Baffled, angry, and thwarted, Sherman vented his contempt on the American settlers, indicting them for their "cowardice" in not driving out the Seminoles themselves, even as he also railed against his troops. Significantly, Sherman was not alone in finding the Seminoles a baffling and infuriating enemy. Desertions among the U. S. Army forces were common, including some by the officer corps. Five thousand troops and officers were engaged in this conflict in Florida, nearly half of all personnel in the U. S. Army at the time. Despite the presence of this large force, the Seminoles were obstinate, persistent, and, in many ways, prevailing. To the great frustration of Washington, they could not be moved out to the western preserves set aside for them beyond the Mississippi. For several years, the Seminoles would hit and run, retreat, and live to fight another day. Conditions were dreadful and took a large toll on the army—indeed, only one in four deaths among the troops was due to combat. The army suspended the fighting for a "summer recess" when the heat became too oppressive and, frequently, the toll too lethal. During this recess all forces withdrew into fixed fortifications. Sherman wrote to his brother John in a letter sent in March 1841 that his solution would be to use larger forces to locate the Seminole encampments and burn them, including their boats and canoes, limiting their means of escape. Sherman's thinking aligned fairly closely with that of Colonel William Jenkins Worth, who at about the same time did away with his troops' summer recess. Despite the tremendous hardships imposed on the government forces by the brutal heat, Worth and his troops raided all summer long, destroying the crops the Seminoles intended to harvest in the fall. Many Seminoles were forced to relent and surrender to the army for transportation west rather than hide out and starve in Florida.

In May 1841 Sherman experienced his highest moment of the war when he was dispatched with orders to escort the Seminole chief Coacoochee or "Wild Cat" to the surrender ceremonies at Fort Pierce. When the handsome young chief arrived at the fort, the negotiations for his and his people's removal west did not go well until Colonel Worth threatened to "string up" the obstinate young leader. Finally relenting, Coacoochee addressed those gathered, describing the treachery and deception he and his people had experienced from the white man.

Promoted in December 1841 to first lieutenant, no doubt quickly because of the high number of desertions, Sherman departed Fort Pierce for his new posting at St. Augustine, the oldest town in the United States. There, his good friend from West Point was in charge, the North Carolinian Braxton Bragg, whom Sherman would later oppose in the Civil War. Sherman had enjoyed his time at Fort Pierce, where he swam in the lagoon and caught tasty fish and turtles for delicious soup and hearty steaks. Still, he now looked forward to being reunited with Bragg. Throughout their lives Sherman remained fond of Bragg despite their conflicts on the battlefield. Sherman would always maintain that Bragg did not have his heart in the rebel cause, but did his duty regardless.

The stint in St. Augustine was short-lived. The Third Artillery was transferred to Fort Moultrie on Sullivan Island, South Carolina, at the entrance to Charleston Harbor. Sherman knew that being stationed at Fort Moultrie with a 250-man garrison overseen by a cadre of brilliant young officers—almost all of whom would achieve distinction two decades later in the Civil War—was a plum assignment. But the fort was not the big attraction. Charleston was. A bustling and prosperous town of nearly thirty thousand, Charleston had charm, comfort, and class to spare. Its society was well established, highly sophisticated, and remarkably well off. For three months, in between the time at Fort Pierce and Fort Moultrie, Sherman had been stationed at Fort Morgan, Alabama, and had frequently traveled the forty miles to Mobile, where he had sampled the graciousness and hospitality of Southern living. Now in Charleston he found it outright intoxicating. He exulted that his status as an officer—sporting the "bright button," as he put it—afforded him instant entrée into high Southern society. He enjoyed its pronounced esteem for the military and its excessively romantic view of those engaged in it—especially officers.

The social whirl was a welcome relief from the crushing ennui of life in the peacetime army. The daily routine at Fort Moultrie was as set and rigid as it had been during the West Point years. But without the classes to attend and the studying to do, the day at the fort was often given over to long intervals between assigned duties. Frequently the men would congregate in Sherman's quarters, for as he had at West Point, he proved himself popular for the four years he served at Fort Moultrie. These months would serve

Sherman well in the future. While at Fort Moultrie he received orders to visit the neighboring states and attend to various supervisory tasks in his capacity as an up-and-coming officer. These assignments took him to Key West, Florida; Augusta, Georgia; North Carolina; and Louisiana. He was sent on a mission that involved touring areas of Georgia and Alabama where he would lead campaigns in twenty years' time. As was his custom, on these trips he studied the terrain closely, especially in Georgia and Alabama.

During the Second Seminole War, he had witnessed first-hand the advantages exploited by the Seminoles due to their vastly superior knowledge of the land. He had also witnessed *celerite*—the speed and efficiency with which the Seminoles struck—devastating the Florida settlers and the unwary army units sent out to hunt for them. Now, with his astonishing visual memory and his uncanny ability to parse topography for the ideal placement of troops, artillery, cavalry, and military fortifications, he was unknowingly preparing for battles yet to come.

Despite the social farrago offered by Charleston—and the number of beautiful Southern belles he danced with at cotillions—Sherman nevertheless kept up an increasingly romantic correspondence with Ellen Ewing. Since he had accumulated the required three years of service in the regular army, he was entitled to obtain a leave of absence. He intended to head straight to Lancaster to find Ellen. In July 1843, he left to spend three months in Ohio with her, but the three months grew to five when the army granted Sherman an extension of two more months in which to resettle his mother, Mary. She could no longer afford her house, despite financial assistance from Sherman and his brothers.

With Ellen, too, there were matters to settle. She was very involved with her family and wanted to remain in and around Lancaster. To Sherman this prospect was absurd. Not only was he now enamored of the South with its elegant social bent and balmy weather, he was also determined to never again be a ward of Tom Ewing.

Given Sherman's adamant convictions on these issues and his insistence on independence and self-sufficiency, one wonders how he came to focus upon his foster sister Ellen, the proverbial apple of the great man's eye. This paradox is especially puzzling considering that Sherman had available to him so many comely young women of the South, free and clear of any complications. Matters of the heart are notoriously tricky, and certainly in Sherman's case they seem illogical.

Ellen had her inexplicable side also. Considering her piety, she couldn't have been pleased with Sherman's belief that God's relationship with humankind is limited to one in which people, if they exercised due charity and sincerity, would attain worldly happiness but nothing more. This brand of atheism showed Sherman's logical side. His theology befits a man raised by lawyers.

Back in Charleston in March 1844, Sherman wrote to Tom Ewing requesting his daughter's hand in marriage. Ewing granted him permission. He and Ellen were engaged, though

they continued to go back and forth with each other over the
three sticking points—family, religion, and an army versus a civil
career—for many years to come, both negotiating and hedging
their commitment. Matters of marriage fell quickly by the wayside
when Congress voted to annex Texas in December 1845. Mexico
disagreed with this unilateral congressional decision and the
Mexican War was on. This opportunity for career advancement
erased for Sherman the possibility of establishing a domestic life
in the American South with a new bride. Dreams of martial glory
trumped thoughts of romantic bliss with Ellen and nearly all other
considerations. Yet participation in the war would prove elusive
for Sherman, try mightily though he did to get into the thick of the
fighting in Texas and in Mexico. First he was assigned to recruiting duty in Pennsylvania and then to active duty in the field, but
in California, where fighting during the Mexican-American War
was peripheral and, compared to the pitched battles in Texas and
Mexico, sporadic and light.

FOUR

California Interlude

Sherman grew restless during the first several months of the Mexican War while he served as a recruiting officer based in Pittsburgh. Being left behind as a desk jockey while his recruits were shipped off to the action agitated him. There were also other troubles. His wedding plans with Ellen were still unsettled. Then, too, his mother's uncertain financial situation was sending shock waves through his family. Foster father Ewing had offered assistance, which bothered Sherman enough to ask his brothers to intervene and help him meet his mother's financial needs. Finally, his older sister Elizabeth was experiencing her own financial crisis, precipitated by her husband's accelerating alcoholism and the damage it was doing to his bank account. All of these factors put Sherman in a vile mood indeed.

Desperate to join the Mexican fight, Sherman accompanied a team of recruits on their journey to Cincinnati, though he had no orders to do so. Once there, he promptly reported to the commanding officer in charge, Colonel Alexander C. W. Fanning, a crusty combat veteran whose battlefield tours of duty had left him with only one arm. Fuming and cursing, Fanning demanded to know what Sherman was doing in Cincinnati. Sherman decamped back to Pittsburgh with his tail between his legs, stopping first for a visit with Ellen in Lancaster.

Sherman's heart soared when he arrived in Pittsburgh on June 26, 1846. He had recently written the adjutant general offering his services for combat duties, and now awaiting him were orders assigning him to Company F, Third Artillery, destined for the wild and disputed territory of California. He hastily put his paperwork in order and dashed off a letter to Ellen, explaining his excitement and his continuing commitment to his army career and imploring her to wait for his return. He then packed his gear and headed once again for Fort Columbus on Governor's Island in New York Harbor. Nervous, excited, and agitated as usual, he was bedeviled by fears that the ship would sail without him. On July 13 the *Lexington* departed, her course mapped around South America by way of the treacherous Cape Horn. She would not reach California until the end of January. Off to war again, Sherman was happy. During the voyage, he marveled at the natural beauty of South America, including Rio de Janeiro's harbor; in Rio he enjoyed the luxurious life of the city. But he deplored the number of free blacks in Rio who were engaged in professions such as law and medicine. He firmly believed all his life that blacks were inferior and should know their place and stay in it.

Next he ventured into Santiago, Chile. In letters to Ellen he had raved about the beauty of the women in Rio, but the raucous bordellos in Santiago appalled him. In his squeamish descriptions of Santiago's houses of ill repute, he sounds prudish, though it is hard to imagine that an army officer wasn't more worldly wise. In any case, his repulsion must have been encouraging to Ellen.

The ship received word en route that the navy had already taken the key port cities in California from the Mexican forces. The Mexican-American War in California was effectively over, despite its fierce continuation in the Southwest and particularly in Texas. Left out of the action once again, Sherman lamented having sailed so far for so many months only to be disappointed. California did nothing to alleviate his depression. He wrote in a letter to his brother John that he would not exchange the entire muddy, undeveloped, and primitive territory for even a few counties of fertile Ohio.

Major Richard B. Mason—Sherman's superior at Fort Moultrie, South Carolina—soon arrived alongside General Stephen W. Kearny to take charge of this wild new territory. Internecine fighting recently had broken out over control of the local government. Remnants of Mexican rule still lingered, and Mexican officials continued to exercise authority in some areas. Because Major Mason had previously assigned Sherman to the recruiting officer's posting in Pittsburgh (in May 1846), Sherman had concluded that Mason disliked him. This proved untrue. Soon Sherman found himself at Mason's right hand, accompanying him in his travels around the territory. Sherman quickly revised his opinion of Mason and came to regard him as an important mentor.

Sherman's overzealous tendencies soon surfaced, though. In his mission to help Mason and Kearny establish law and order he turned his energies toward John H. Nash, an older *alcalde*, or regional government officer under the Mexican system of government. For three months Nash insisted on preserving his legitimately entitled elected office, against the orders of the new government. Sherman organized a raiding party, stormed into the Sonoma house where Nash was enjoying dinner, forcefully removed him, and transported him via boat to Monterey. There Sherman watched the badly weakened and fearful old man's abject capitulation to Mason.

Sherman little suspected the development that was about to influence his career profoundly. In early spring 1848, James Marshall, a veteran of service in Fremont's California Battalion, noticed something glinting from a ditch. Marshall was building a water-powered sawmill on the American Fork River for a land-owner and entrepreneur named Johann Augustus Sutter. Sutter dug up some of the ore and sent samples to Mason's office for identification. In fact, it was William Tecumseh Sherman who confirmed that gold had been found in California. He had memo-rized the distinctive properties of basic minerals while at West Point and knew what Sutter had. The California Gold Rush began.

The Forty-niners poured into the territory in numbers exceeding a hundred thousand. Men abandoned their wives, children, farms, fields, crops, and animals—everything—and lit out to pan for gold. Entire towns were deserted. San Francisco essentially emptied. Soldiers from the U. S. Army deserted en masse, as did sailors from U. S. Navy ships, many of which were left moored dockside or in the harbors without even a skeleton crew sufficient to move them.

The whole territory of California, followed by seemingly the entire country, caught gold fever, and the equivalent of a feeding frenzy was loosed. Mason and Sherman twice visited the upper American River gold fields—once in July and again in September—and filed official reports that they dispatched back to Washington attesting to the breadth and veracity of this vast strike. News of the strike's magnitude spread to Europe. It was a once-in-a-lifetime opportunity that stirred up deep anxieties in Sherman. He started itching to capitalize on the surrounding bonanza, and on the second visit he paid to the gold fields with Mason, he devised a scheme whereby the two of them plus Lieutenant William H. Warner would be partners in a general store in Coloma.

They used Warner's clerk, Norman S. Bestor, to front the store as sole owner. Rumors circulated that Mason was stocking the store with misappropriated government supplies. With inflation running so high, a killing was there for the making. As it turned out, the three partners reaped a fifteen-hundred-dollar profit each on their initial investment of five hundred dollars apiece. The threefold return on their initial investment was somewhat worthwhile but piddling compared to the windfalls made by lucky prospectors.

Sherman was left with ambivalent feelings. The promise of his California experience was quickly eroding. On the one hand, he wanted to resign his commission and leave the army for a chance at big money, satisfying Ellen's wishes. On the other hand, the Mexican War ended with the United States' triumph and with California achieving statehood.

Now that the war was over, Sherman predicted the army would experience severe cuts to its funding by Congress. That meant it was likely his resignation would be rapidly and gratefully accepted. Because of a new mail service via steamship, Sherman was in more frequent communication with Ellen. But these letter exchanges with her only added to his misery. She complained to him of poor health and went so far as to suggest that he consider courting a younger and more vital woman. This Sherman protested and disclaimed any interest in doing. Still, their serious differences persisted over the contentious issues of religion, over army service versus the professions or private enterprise, over financial stability and how best to attain it, and over how and when they would align themselves with the Ewing family.

Fortuitously, Sherman was assigned a mission that put him back in the action. Twenty-eight newly arrived soldiers from the Second Infantry Division had deserted with gold in their eyes and Sherman was to rein the miscreants in. In no time he was leading a charge across the Salinas River, trapping most of the escapees in an adobe ranch house. With his ruthless efficiency, Sherman corralled all the deserters like so many wayward cows and brought them back to suffer army justice.

Sherman, overqualified for such petty assignments, had

rapidly completed his mission. It was as near as Sherman ever came to dangerous action in California, aside from the ambush and abduction of hapless old Nash. Neither action was the type that garnered medals or promotions. It is easy, therefore, to understand the sense of deflation that overtook Sherman when he opened the newspaper soon thereafter and learned that Major Mason, who had been rotated back to Washington, had been promoted to brigadier general. Sherman was proud of his former superior officer and knew that Mason had done nothing to justify any feelings of envy, but by missing the battlefield action during the war, Sherman feared that he had forfeited all chance of having a successful army career. Now he felt truly left behind. He confided his misgivings to General Edmund Kirby Smith, who dissuaded him from too negative a view of things and guaranteed him a trip back East to deliver reports and dispatches, as long as he didn't resign.

In fact, Smith would have him report directly to General in Chief of the Army Winfield Scott. Skeptical as ever, Sherman agreed nonetheless. While he waited for Smith to pull together the appropriate paperwork for the trip back East, Sherman attended the California constitutional convention as Smith's emissary. Predictably the scheming, infighting, greed, and jockeying for preference and power appalled him. He did, however, find the debate over slavery piquant, though it didn't affect his views. He remained as proslavery as ever.

After taking time for a celebratory New Year's dinner at his boarding house in Monterey, Sherman left for New York aboard the steamship *Oregon*. He had for company his old friend and West Point classmate E. O. C. Ord, and along for the trip as well were California's two inaugural senators, William M. Gwin and the feisty John C. Fremont. The once again disgruntled Sherman departed the newly founded Golden State three years after he first arrived there. He was severely unimpressed with himself and quite apprehensive about whether his future held any promise at all.

FIVE

Captain and Married Man

UPON ARRIVAL IN New York City at the end of January 1850, Sherman quickly hurried to the office of Winfield Scott. Highly polished and always formal, the commanding General of the Army was extraordinarily decorous, hence the nickname "Old Fuss and Feathers." Sherman politely and professionally began describing matters out West in California. General Scott, however, was preoccupied. After briefly volunteering his views on California, he stunned the young first lieutenant by proclaiming his belief that the country was moving swiftly toward civil war. He then invited Sherman to dine with him that evening. Awestruck, Sherman accepted immediately.

This must have been a heady privilege for a young offi-cer. Scott had achieved international fame as the hero of the

Mexican-American War. In turn, the old officer no doubt wanted to treat Sherman with the utmost respect—even favor—because Scott harbored political ambitions and was eyeing the upcoming Whig nomination for president. Thus, a sturdy relationship with the powerful Tom Ewing, who was currently serving as secretary of interior for President Zachary Taylor, would be most useful. Scott was so impressed with Sherman's briefing on the situation in California that he sent him directly to Washington to report to President Taylor and Secretary of War George W. Crawford. Sherman was only too happy to do this. Not only was a meeting with the president of the United States at the White House an exciting opportunity, but also Tom Ewing and his family, including Ellen, were at that time living across the street at Blair House. Sherman hastened to the capital and, after a rather droll meeting with the secretary of war, had an hour's meeting with President Taylor. Sherman was surprised to find the president more relaxed and easier to talk to than the starchy Winfield Scott.

Having completed the assignment designated to him by General Smith in California, Sherman was pleased when his superiors granted him a leave of six months for a job well done. Sherman visited with the entire Ewing family and then spent some time alone with Ellen, who insisted that he consider returning with her to Lancaster to live, raise a family, and work for her father in his salt works. The idea of working for Tom Ewing was abhorrent to Sherman, having benefited since age nine from his foster father's magnanimity and wishing mightily, as Sherman did, to free himself of any further indebtedness. Ironically, by staying in Washington and visiting such high-ranking army figures as the adjutant general, Sherman had to be aware that he was capitalizing on his foster father's elite status. Perhaps as a response to this psychological turmoil, Sherman focused hard yet again on independently making something of himself. At that very moment Congress was considering the creation of four new captaincies in the commissary division, and Sherman advanced himself eagerly as one of the most deserving first lieutenants. He pointed out that he had sacrificed chances for advancement by serving loyally in California while many of his cohorts worked to advance their careers through combat service. He even underscored that he had performed admirably under both Mason and Smith, yet had been denied promotion when Mason was elevated, which was highly unorthodox since an adjutant usually received a promotion simultaneously with his superior officer.

In the meantime, Sherman proceeded with his marriage to his foster sister. It was quite the social event, drawing the crème de la crème of Washington society, including President Taylor and his cabinet, justices from the Supreme Court, high-ranking diplomats, and congressmen such as Tom Ewing's long-standing friends Daniel Webster and Henry Clay. Held at Blair House, the evening wedding ceremony on May 1, 1850, was a spectacularly lavish affair. Tom Ewing spared no expense in giving away his oldest daughter. Ellen and her mother were disappointed that the ceremony was not centered on a formal Catholic nuptial mass, but Sherman, of course, had not wanted this formal religious aspect. He was, nevertheless, sensitive enough to his wife's wishes that he had two Catholic friends serve as groomsmen. Following the ceremony William and Ellen set off on their honeymoon,

accompanied by Ellen's younger brother, Tom. The three traveled from Philadelphia, New York, and West Point to Niagara
Falls, Buffalo, and Lancaster, visiting friends and family along
the way. They remained in Lancaster for a month, where Ellen's
older brother Phil, Sherman's boyhood sidekick, took the couple
on a tour of the Chauncey salt works, probably in the misplaced
hope that Sherman would perhaps be interested in working there
one day. Sherman remained dead set against it. During their honeymoon Ellen received a number of letters from her parents in
Washington, informing her that they already missed her severely,
and how very pleased they would be if the new couple agreed to
come to Washington and establish a home there not far from Blair
House. This entreaty would resound throughout their marriage,
causing friction for many years to come. But at least now, after
the five-year engagement with its endless negotiation and debate,
William and Ellen were married, although both were less than
sure about the future.

Thanks to a promise General Winfield Scott made to Tom
Ewing, Sherman was finally promoted to captain that coming
September, just before President Taylor fell ill and died. This
shocking turn of events lost Ewing his cabinet post, and he immediately filled a vacant seat for Ohio in the Senate. As for Sherman,
he spent the rest of his leave of absence observing the congressional debates surrounding the Compromise of 1850, legislation that
stipulated which states and new territories would permit slavery
and later, in essence, expanded the territorial range of the Civil
War. Sherman's own views had not changed. Like Tom Ewing, he
was a staunch Whig, proslavery without a single scruple. He still

believed in the manifest destiny of the white race and the inferiority of African Americans and Native Americans.

Sherman was soon posted to St. Louis, much to the chagrin
of Ellen and her parents. He remembered St. Louis from previous
journeys and was pleased with the assignment. He admired the
city's sense of industry and destiny as a gateway to the West. The
disagreement with Ellen and the Ewings became moot shortly
after Sherman arrived alone in St. Louis to secure lodgings and
learned that Ellen, who had stayed behind in Lancaster, was preg-
nant. He then reluctantly agreed with Ellen's plans—proposed by
her parents—for her to remain in Lancaster until the child was
born.

Sherman put his chagrined feelings aside and applied himself
with diligence to his new duties. When these duties left him with
considerable amounts of time on his hands, he began looking
after Tom Ewing's substantial business interests in and around
St. Louis, which were heavily vested in real estate and land. In all
these business affairs, Sherman proved himself a prudent manager and adviser, giving his father-in-law accurate estimates of
the worth of his assets as well as sage advice on when to buy or
sell. He also found time to write often to Ellen, extolling the pro-
gressive charms of St. Louis and underscoring its large Catholic
population and the considerable number of Catholic churches
presided over by an ample cadre of educated priests.

Happily, Ellen wrote to inform her husband that he was the
father of a healthy daughter, born on January 28, 1851. The
child was promptly baptized a Catholic and named in honor
of her maternal grandmother, Maria. Like so many Ewings

who answered only to nicknames, the newly christened Maria responded all of her life to "Minnie." Two months later, Sherman traveled to Lancaster and brought his wife and young daughter to St. Louis, installing the family in a modest house on Chouteau Avenue. Ellen missed her family and their comfortable accommodations in Lancaster almost immediately. Worse, she wasn't as taken with St. Louis and its booming prospects as her husband was. He was also more comfortable within their new circle of acquaintances than she, composed as it was mostly of fellow army officers and their wives, though it wasn't long before he began to fret and fuss over the strain of providing for a family on a soldier's moderate salary.

Despite some welcomed stability brought about by a new friendship with Major Henry S. Turner and his wife, with whom Sherman had served in Monterey, the Shermans were still uneasy, as there were rumors that the new captain would soon be transferred out of town. This indeed proved to be true, but first Sherman suffered a huge blow. His mother died unexpectedly. This came as quite a shock, for her recent letters had assured him of her good health. It was a sad season for Sherman, who, in a later letter to his wife characterized his mother's life as one of too much hardship and pain.

When Sherman received temporary orders to report to Fort Leavenworth, Kansas, on urgent army business, he decided to economize, sending a disgruntled and homesick Ellen back to Lancaster with their daughter in the summer of 1852. New orders arrived for him that autumn: he was to report to New Orleans and clean up a mess in the commissary department caused by an incompetent officer. Sherman reported to New Orleans in October and quickly set about the task of setting matters straight, careful not to take undue retributive actions against the officer he was replacing. Sherman liked New Orleans and settled in to an active social life, much of it with fellow officers but a considerable amount spent with civilians, who appreciated the cleanup job he had done. Two drawbacks prevented him from being truly happy: he was once again separated from his family, and he was finding New Orleans even more expensive than St. Louis. Sherman's unhappiness subsided when Ellen wrote to tell him that he was a father for a second time, his daughter Mary Elizabeth having been born on November 17, 1852. He must have been doubly thrilled that the new daughter would be named Mary Elizabeth, after his recently departed mother and his favorite eldest sister.

In late December, Ellen and the two girls joined him, having made the journey from Ohio with his sister Fanny who was along both to help and because Sherman thought the trip would ease Fanny's grief over the recent loss of their mother. He achieved a brief season of contentment upon their arrival, which was unfortunately very short-lived. Again, Ellen was not happy in reduced circumstances. Her need for three servants proved an insufferable strain on her husband's resources. For a second time he saw that his income was not able to meet his expenses. Ellen, sometimes aided by her father, continued to implore her husband to quit his army career and pursue his fortune in private enterprise.

Henry Turner, who had become a prosperous banker back in St. Louis, was of the same mind. Turner pointed out to Sherman that the experience he had acquired during his California tour of duty, added to the management skills he had demonstrated as a commissary officer, and, finally, the supervisory and consulting services he had provided for his father-in-law made Sherman a natural candidate for banking. Turner then disclosed to Sherman that he and his partners, Lucas, Simmonds and Company, were in the process of opening a branch office in San Francisco. Would an offer of partnership *and* salary hold any interest for Sherman? Turner proved he meant business by adding a diversionary stop-over in New Orleans for a face-to-face meeting with Sherman on the way to New York.

Events gained a momentum of their own. Turner went on to New York and, after completing his business there, made a hasty side trip to Washington to secure Sherman a six-month leave of absence in order to try out the proposed position. The lead partner, James Lucas, traveled to New Orleans to interview Sherman. The deal was done: by the end of February, Sherman had secured an annual salary of five thousand dollars and a one-eighth partnership. With his usual decisiveness, Sherman dispatched Ellen, their two daughters, and his sister Fanny back to Ohio. Then he sold the house and its contents via auction.

Over the years Sherman had kept in contact with many of the friends he had made during his military service in California, so he wrote ahead announcing his imminent arrival. When Sherman boarded a ship in New Orleans on March 6 bound for San Francisco, he was hopeful that his move to the Golden State would result in a suitable financial condition. Finally he could provide for his family as Ellen expected him to. As he left

St. Louis in March 1853 bound for California for a second time, Sherman was quite bullish on his commercial prospects as compared to his army realities, although he had hedged his bet by not resigning his army commission.

Portrait of Major General Sherman. This photograph was taken in 1865 by Matthew Brady.

This 1881 painting by James E. Taylor was a gift to Sherman from the artist. It is called "Before Five Forks, Sheridan at Dinwiddie Court House." It depicts General Philip Sheridan, with his cavalry leaders, George Custer, Wesley Merritt, T. C. Devin, and George Crook, about to leave Headquarters at Dinwiddie Court House on March 31st 1865, to reconnoiter Five Forks. In the foreground is a field hand describing topography of the country around the Forks. Confederate cavalry prisoners and the Court House are in the background.

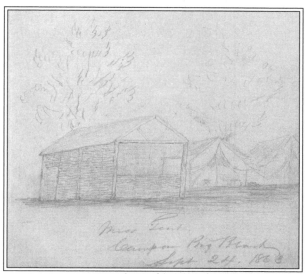

Sketch of tents in camp on the Big Black River near
Vicksburg, Mississippi, by William Tecumseh Sherman,
dated September 24, 1868.

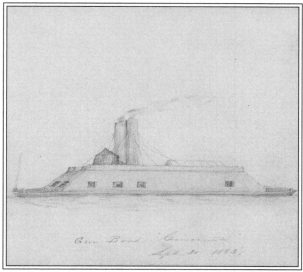

Sketch of the gun boat "Cincinnati" on the Mississippi
River near Vicksburg by William Tecumseh Sherman;
dated September 30, 1883

SIX

The Middle Passage

THE HAZARDS OF travel in the nineteenth century are virtually unimaginable for Americans today. On April 9, 1853, within a day's sailing of San Francisco, Sherman was asleep in a deck chair when his steamer struck a reef in the darkness. The awakened passengers panicked, but without hesitation Sherman, a highly nervous man under normal circumstances, proved steady and sure of himself and helped to calm the other passengers so that they could be off-loaded to small boats and taken safely to land. Sherman hopped into one of the small boats and in the morning was on a schooner heading up the coast to San Francisco. When the schooner entered the San Francisco Bay, foul weather tossed it and turned it on its side. Fortunately, Sherman managed to catch the attention of a small passing vessel, the fourth he had sailed on within twenty-four hours, which, at last, took him ashore.

As Sherman neared his debut in the world of private enterprise, he was taken aback by the dramatic transformation the city of San Francisco had undergone in the three years since he had left. Thanks to the gold rush, he now saw a city of substantial houses, impressive banks, government buildings, and sturdy churches. No longer were there small wooden houses flanking muddy streets. Now there were some fifty thousand residents filling a prosperous city and a harbor crowded with the spars of merchant ships bringing in supplies and luxury goods for the residents of the new metropolis.

All of this was exciting to Sherman, and he was elated until he met with Turner. Only one hundred thousand dollars had been allocated to the new bank branch, one-third of what Sherman believed it should have been. He also found the bank office extremely unimpressive. Despite these two shortcomings, Sherman threw himself into the banking business with his usual intelligence and energy. Soon he had investigated every aspect of the bank's operation and had schooled himself thoroughly on even the smallest details. He also set about the task of making himself well-known and well-liked in the community. When the head partner finally agreed to double the capitalization of Sherman's branch to two hundred thousand dollars, Sherman became most optimistic about the bank's future, as well as his own.

Once again the family was to be relocated, this time to San Francisco. When Sherman visited Lancaster to fetch his family for the journey back to California, he proudly conveyed to his father-in-law his success so far and the promise of his future. Tom was pleased but had a proposition Sherman wasn't entirely happy with. He and Maria were lonely for a child's presence and entreated William and Ellen to leave Minnie behind. Ellen agreed, as did, eventually, a reluctant Sherman.

Sherman must also have been sad at the end of that summer to write his letter of resignation from the army. The military career he had launched seventeen years earlier with his climb up the winding road from the wharf to the plains at West Point was now seemingly at an end, having achieved no great distinction, having bequeathed no lasting legacy. It is hard to imagine Sherman posting this letter without a sense of ambivalence about what he was giving up, no matter how great the prospects that lay before him as a prosperous banker.

He then took a ship from New York bound for San Francisco with Ellen, Lizzie, and Lizzie's nurse in tow. They sailed without incident and upon arrival the family settled into a large, spacious house at a good address in San Francisco. Sherman proceeded hastily to furnish and staff it, confident of his financial future.

At first this confidence proved justified. Ellen was pleasantly surprised by her new standard of living, and the meager days of army postings seemed well behind them. There was a large Catholic population in San Francisco, and Ellen made friends with a bishop who was eventually elevated to archbishop. This was all very important to Ellen, despite Sherman's indifference. She oversaw Lizzie's upbringing and education brilliantly, and was even able—much to her delight—to place her in parochial schools. This was fine with her husband, as long as he was free to go horseback riding on Sunday mornings while his wife and daughter marched off to mass.

Things would soon change, however. Because the economy of San Francisco was thriving, credit was in much demand. Sherman clearly had the vision and the managerial skills to be a successful banker, yet lacked the required temperament and personality. Popular as he was with the merchant class, they took their business to his competitors because of Sherman's conservative policies in dealing with overdraft privileges. No matter how secure and prosperous the borrower, Sherman would extend only so much credit. Eventually this hurt him and hurt his bank.

His memories of his natural father's debt and ruin were not easily forgotten. Moreover, his sense of order led him to dun even the more modest female owners of boarding houses should they fall behind. Indeed, he would do this himself, strolling about town and knocking on doors. Many San Franciscans found this behavior unseemly for the head of a bank.

Financial disaster struck in 1854 when a big run hit the largest bank in San Francisco, damaging its bottom line extensively. Sherman somehow did not anticipate that the next day his bank, too, would experience a run, but luckily he was able to meet the demands of every depositor wishing to withdraw funds. This was mainly because Sherman's army friends provided him with additional government funds, in what amounted to an early instance of a bailout by the federal government. When the crisis was over, Sherman repaid his army friends the funds they had advanced him. It is significant that the army, whose security Sherman had been most reluctant to give up, proved to be his salvation at this critical time.

Two years later, Sherman found himself in a position that was worse than the bank run in many ways. The governor of California had appointed him the head of the state militia, granting him the rank of major general. He appreciated this until in the spring of 1856 matters became quite messy. A policeman and a prominent publisher were murdered. Grief grew into rage and soon a large vigilante group arose and demanded that those suspected of the murders be put to death immediately. The governor instructed Sherman to call out the militia and quash any nascent civil unrest. Though he was a fervent proponent of law and order, Sherman conducted himself with great reserve in the midst of accusations of a perceived lack of courage and sense of justice. He promptly resigned as head of the militia, answered his critics publicly, and found himself heatedly embroiled with politicians and members of the press, both of whom heaped caustic criticism on him. For the rest of his life Sherman nurtured a deep dislike of politicians and the press. This aversion explains why, years later, he adamantly refused to be drafted for public office, even for the presidency.

Events progressively worsened. The California economy was hideously depressed in the aftermath of the gold rush. As a result, in January 1857, senior partner James Lucas instructed Sherman to begin closing the San Francisco branch of their operation. Sherman rapidly rolled up the operation and took Ellen and his family by ship to New York, where Lucas had invited him to open a Manhattan branch of the bank. It can't have been easy for

Sherman to give up California. He liked the state by now and had become accustomed to the status he had earned in the business and social circles of San Francisco. It also appealed to him that he was a continent removed from the Ewings in Lancaster, Ohio.

While in California—in June 1854 and October 1855—Ellen had borne William two sons, Willy and Tom. Sherman reacted more enthusiastically to their births than he had to the births of his two girls.

Even compared to most nineteenth-century fathers, Sherman had been emphatically remote from his children until the West Coast years. But during those years in San Francisco he wrote of the pleasure he took in his children and in the mischief they got into, exploring rooms and closets and drawers in their large and comfortable house. He saw Minnie only on visits back to Lancaster, where she lived with her Ewing grandparents, but Lizzie and the two boys were with him in the San Francisco household and this seemed to please him greatly. He boasted incessantly about his sons, especially about firstborn Willy, on whom he doted.

New York was a business venue that Sherman was willing to try, though he feared attempting to keep up with the New York "sharpies," as he referred to Gotham's slick wheelers and dealers in one of his letters. Considering the alternative of returning to Lancaster and going to work in his father-in-law's salt works, the rat race of Wall Street seemed worth an attempt. He had once confided to a friend that he hated the very idea of returning to

Lancaster, where he would "only be Cump Sherman." No one valued stature and distinction in the community more than did Sherman. He had told Ellen numerous times in his letters of his wish to achieve fame and military glory, no doubt as compensation for what he saw as his childhood humiliations.

Upon his arrival in New York, Sherman promptly shipped his family to Lancaster yet again, while he tested the possibilities of Manhattan. No sooner had he opened the Lucas branch office in Lower Manhattan at 12 Wall Street than the Panic of 1857 set in. Oddly enough, one of the precipitating forces behind this panic was the wreck of the *Central America*, the same ship that had pleasantly transported the Shermans to New York from San Francisco four months earlier. The ship went down on its way to New York from San Francisco, sinking off the coast of North Carolina, and took with it several tons of California gold, as well as everyone on board.

Many teetering New York banks had been counting on this gold specie from California to shore up their sinking reserves. When the ship sank, so did many New York banks, which numbered at about sixty—far more than were needed. Most of the banks that failed had issued more paper than they had reserves to back it with. When runs on the banks inevitably came, the depositors could not be reimbursed and the financial bubble burst. The sinking of the *Central America* was one of the most famous losses for American shipping in all of the nineteenth century, as well as one of the most consequential. It was a sad time for Sherman.

In October he salvaged what assets he could from the Wall Street office and took them to his company's headquarters in St.

Louis to organize. This process took through the end of the year to complete. In January 1858, he made a trip to San Francisco to tie up the loose ends that still dangled there, as well as to sell his former home at a 40 percent loss. He returned to St. Louis in July to settle with Lucas and his other partners and to part ways with them. Admirably, Sherman made up out of his own pocket a shortfall of fifteen thousand dollars owed to the army officers in San Francisco who had invested with him, seeing to it personally that they lost not so much as a penny. Still, feelings of failure must have haunted him.

As Sherman lamented in a letter to a friend, he found himself back in Lancaster that August with his family, out of work, and, worst of all, dependent once again on Tom Ewing. Sherman's anguish is not hard to imagine. Resigning from the army must have seemed then precipitous and foolish. He tried to get his brother John, a congressman now, to have him reinstated in the army, but there were no openings during this time of economic turmoil and military peace. Tom Ewing offered his son-in-law employment yet again in his salt works. Sherman predictably declined and wrote to his foster brother Tom Ewing Jr. offering his services as an office manager for Tom's prosperous law firm in Leavenworth, Kansas. Sherman mentioned that he was on the market "cheap." Sherman got the job and headed west, leaving his family behind in Lancaster. This was now a familiar scenario and suited Ellen perfectly.

For his part, Sherman was happy to be in Leavenworth, hardly more than a village that had grown up around a large fort and as a consequence was dependent on the army for its existence.

On one hand, being in close proximity to army officers cheered Sherman, who knew many of them stationed there, but it also increased Sherman's regret that he was no longer among them.

Initially Sherman worked as an office manager, but he was soon elevated to membership in the Kansas bar after inquiring from a local circuit judge what would be necessary for him to qualify as a lawyer. After a brief chat, the judge pronounced him qualified "on the ground of general intelligence." Thus Sherman became a barrister in the Kansas Territory as well as in the "North Western Counties of Missouri." Tom Ewing Jr.'s law firm promptly changed its name to "Sherman and Ewing" and immediately printed up business cards to that effect. Sherman appeared in court twice, lost twice, and exited completely disgusted with courtroom theatrics and chicanery. To his credit, Sherman later joked at his own expense about his ineptness as a lawyer, just as he had disparaged himself a few years earlier as the "Jonah of banking."

That he was honest about his failings in both fields of endeavor is not surprising. He prized neither field of endeavor as a career, always knowing that his real career lay in the army life he loved. He remarked that being so close to Fort Leavenworth made him feel "perfectly at home with sound of bugle and drum." His distaste for politicians, lawyers, and members of the press was legendary; and in an era when banking was completely unregulated, he often declared that banking and gambling were "synonymous terms."

Sherman pulled every political string he could think of in

an attempt to be reinstated in the army when he learned that a vacancy existed in the Pay Department. All attempts failed, principally because Pennsylvania Democrat James Buchanan occupied the White House as president, and Tom Ewing Sr. had been a lifelong leader of the Whigs, chief opponents of the Democrats. Under the stress of all these setbacks, Sherman grew increasingly depressed, but still angrily refused to accept a position back in Ohio working for his father-in-law.

Sherman retreated to the one-room farmhouse—hardly more than a shack—that sat on Tom Ewing's Kansas property. Sherman lived there under rough conditions, a former high-ranking bank executive and before that a respected captain in the U. S. Army, reduced to the level of a sharecropper. Understandably, Sherman was despondent, racked with depression at what he perceived to be his utter failure. The constant family pressure to surrender to the will of his father-in-law also tormented him. Not a man to give up easily, Tom Ewing offered Sherman a new job as manager of a bank he and other Ohioans planned to open in London. Lucas also offered Sherman another banking position in San Francisco. Disappointed at not being recommissioned as an army officer, Sherman was tempted by these offers, yet his two previous banking failures worried him. The last thing he wanted was to pronounce himself the "Jonah of banking" again, especially if Tom Ewing was involved.

Then a particularly interesting job prospect came along. The army buddies with whom Sherman had been in touch concerning the vacancy in the army's Pay Department let him know about a superintendent position at a new military academy in Louisiana.

It so happened that Sherman's old commanding officer, Richard B. Mason, had a half brother named G. Mason Graham on the new academy's board. Intrigued by a job that would at least be quasi-military, Sherman wrote a long and sparkling letter applying for the job. Although several members of the board had understandable reservations about Sherman being a native of Ohio, a state rife with abolitionists, they soon learned they had nothing to worry about with this particular applicant and elected to appoint Sherman to the position.

Even so, Sherman hesitated slightly before accepting. Although he wanted the superintendent's job, he wanted to be reinstated directly into the army even more. Hastily, he made one last trip to Washington to appeal in person for the Pay Department opening—but to no avail. With no other options other than repeated offers from his father-in-law, Sherman accepted the job in Louisiana, assuming it would give him and his family security and a permanent home—one sufficiently distant from Tom and Maria Ewing. Happy to be out from under the crushing weight of near total failure, Sherman looked forward to leaving the hardscrabble shack on the Kansas plains and to having many happy years in Louisiana as a superintendent and professor of engineering, drawing, and architecture.

SEVEN

Superintendent

IN OCTOBER HE set out for Louisiana, traveling down the Mississippi by paddle wheeler, a bucolic experience that inspired moving scenes in the stories of Samuel Clemens. But the peace ended when Sherman reached the site of the new school. He was disappointed in its isolated setting in the piney woods. It was thirty-five hours from New Orleans and so remote that mail deliveries took weeks. This delay was torture for a dedicated letter writer. The physical condition of the school was also disappointing. Only the main building was complete, along with one faculty house, which had already been commandeered by a colleague. Not only was the main building lacking furniture, but the superintendent's house assigned to the Shermans was only in the early stages of construction, with completion not expected for months.

Undaunted, Sherman threw himself into the task of making the Louisiana State Seminary of Learning and Military Academy a first-rate institution. He became fast friends with General George Mason Graham and divided duties between themselves. Researching other military academies and appropriating their best features was first on the agenda. Sherman wrote to his superintendent at West Point, Major Delafield, and received his input and advice. Thanks to his army buddies, Sherman also knew that a young and ambitious West Point graduate named George McClellan had recently made an inspection tour of Europe's leading military schools in search of ideas to be applied at West Point. So Sherman wrote to him for his recommendations also. In addition, Sherman paid a visit to a military school in Kentucky and Graham toured the Virginia Military Institute. After briefing the new academy's board on what he and Graham had discovered, Sherman wrote a prospectus for the new school, now housed in the library at LSU, the great institution that evolved from this academy. In January 1860, the academy managed to open on schedule, thanks to Sherman hastily purchasing texts from New York City, having found no supplier in the South able to fill his orders. This and other strategic decisions, such as commissioning a tailor from Manhattan to make uniforms for the new cadets, did not sit well with some of the members of the board. This was indicative of the national mood at the time; the academy board resented anything Sherman purchased outside of the South.

The cadets themselves posed a considerable problem. Sherman, vigilant and alert, had thought to advertise the opening of the school, but the response from applicants at first fell far short of what had been hoped for. Therefore the standards had to be lowered. This meant lesser academic credentials and diminished physical standards like age and height. The other problem with the Louisiana Seminary cadets, which had been anticipated by Sherman, concerned their demeanor, attitude, and level of discipline. Unlike cadets at West Point, the Louisiana cadets did not receive a full government-funded scholarship. And, unlike cadets at VMI—the Virginia Military Institute—who adhered to a strict military code of behavior enforced by a court-martial system, the cadets under Sherman's charge, in his opinion, were given far too much leeway.

The school's faculty, particularly the superintendent, lacked the means to enforce order and proper behavior. This lack of disciplinary authority proved to be an essential mistake and brought Sherman into conflict with the parents of cadets he did discipline, especially when he expelled them from the school. Sherman's cadets had been drawn almost exclusively from the rich planter class of Louisiana. They were spoiled and headstrong, having grown accustomed to dominating slaves rather than doing arduous work for themselves. They did not take well to rules and discipline imposed on them and Sherman was regarded as far too strict, harsh, arbitrary, and inflexible. Just as the merchants of San Francisco had found him too punitive to deal with comfortably, so the academy students would bristle under his harsh rule. The board sometimes stepped into the breach to mollify the superintendent's rulings. This interference didn't sit well with Major Sherman, as he was now titled, though in his army career he had only attained the rank of captain. Still, he knew when to defer and when to hold his ground. He had grown in finesse and polish. Having no other prospects for employment, he had no intention of losing his academy job through bravado and pique.

Opportunities for other employment did appear. The banking job was again presented to Sherman by his Ewing relatives. The high salary was tempting. Shrewdly, Sherman conveyed this attractive offer to the academy's board and received in return a substantial, though far from matching, increase in salary. The leveraging move worked for him: he avoided any family indebtedness and retained his quasi-military status at the academy.

A crisis for Sherman and his Louisiana future had been stewing for quite some time. In the early months of 1860, the South already seethed with rebellion. The previous October, John Brown and his band took hostages and raided the government arsenal at Harpers Ferry, West Virginia, causing a bloody shootout with U. S. Marines under the command of Brevet Colonel Robert E. Lee. This was the first time a white abolitionist had used violence to further the cause and the incident had both inflamed and terrified the South, now intent upon calling up the state militias. According to Southern thinking at the time, this call-up was necessary in anticipation of more raids by Northern abolitionists who would perhaps imitate Brown. Though the South condemned Brown and his marauders as thieves attempting to shatter law and order, the North viewed them as misguided, idealistic martyrs for an honorable cause. Bellicose feelings in the South ran high, as did paranoia and hostility toward all things of the North. Some of these hostile feelings toward the North were inevitably aimed at Sherman, a native of Ohio. Making matters worse, Sherman's congressman brother John had unwittingly endorsed a book that ardently advocated abolition: John R. Helper's *Impending Crisis of the South*. This suspicion of Sherman was misguided. Sherman held no tolerance for abolition, regarding slavery as an appropriate fate for blacks. After all, he came directly from the ultraconservative Whig Party. Sherman even urged Ellen to consider buying a slave when she did join him in Louisiana because she preferred such a lifestyle and also because conditions at the academy were so primitive that no white servants from the North would abide them. Sherman's diplomatic skills—and his proslavery views—helped him defuse the hostility directed toward him. In addition he suggested to his congressman brother that he be more circumspect about his public stance and the endorsement of books. Matters settled down—for a season.

Sherman flourished in his academy role. Despite the loneliness, he was happy in Louisiana and the cadets grew to love him after they became accustomed to his often gruff demeanor. Above all, they liked that he instituted dances with young ladies recruited from nearby schools and put on fun-filled holiday celebrations. He also led a Friday night storytelling session that proved most popular, especially when he regaled the cadets with vivid tales of gold rush California during the height of the hysteria. Because of limited time, Sherman could not yet teach the advanced courses in engineering and architecture, but this weekly storytelling hour afforded him a mentor role with his charges and endeared him to them.

William Tecumseh Sherman, despite hardship and failure—indeed, perhaps because of them—had finally found his niche. If events had continued uninterrupted, Sherman might have built an enduring legacy of educational leadership and family matters might have settled down for him. The esteem and prosperity he dreamed of might have been his. But it was not to be.

When news arrived one afternoon in late December of the secession of South Carolina, Sherman's extreme reaction proved entirely appropriate. Because he knew that South Carolina had precipitated war, he wept openly. Pacing his office while admonishing a colleague, a teacher of classics and a secessionist from Virginia, he insisted that the South knew nothing of the horrors of war. Southerners did not understand, he said, that an agrarian people could never defeat a region of mechanical advancement. The war would be devastating for the romantic South, with its misguided military ideals based on outmoded and outgunned chivalry. The greatest tragedy of American history was about to begin. Sherman's vision of his great country drowning in a savage bloodbath was not delusional. It would indeed happen, and with horrifying rapidity. The immediate consequences of South Carolina's secession were not long in coming. In the following days, other Southern states followed South Carolina and seceded. Louisiana declared its independence from the union on January 26, 1861. Sherman's heart sank. There was no hope now that he could continue as superintendent of the academy. By seceding from the union, the state of Louisiana had cut the ground from under him. He would spend the next month in an uncomfortable situation.

He was sure he would resign, but, ever the pragmatic he knew that if he did so immediately, he would forfeit the salary increase he had won by leveraging the recent banking offer. His salary increase was to arrive as a lump sum bonus once the state legislature approved it, but that hadn't happened yet. Sherman was determined to await this approval and leave with his pockets full, especially since he was again moving into an uncertain future. Ellen urged him to return to Ohio and work for her father. In response William set about exploring a return to California to yet again seek his fortune there. It was an unsettling time.

Sherman's safety was also at stake, at least according to repeated warnings issued by his entire family. The governor of Louisiana designated the academy as a state arsenal and commandeered weapons and ammunition from existing federal arsenals within the state and stored them at the academy. Sherman regarded such actions as treasonous and sought as soon as possible to disassociate himself from any connection to the unlawful actions. His bonus came through in late February and he resigned. Though reluctantly, the board accepted his resignation and issued him a letter of commendation for the job he had done. In saying goodbye to his cadets, Sherman became emotional and tapping his chest told them that they would always have a place in his heart. Such an emotional public display was quite remarkable for a man of his nature, whose emotional depth was considered by many as shallow at best.

In making his way back to Lancaster, Ohio, Sherman traveled first to New Orleans. There, his good friend Braxton Bragg informed him that he believed there would be no war. Sherman knew better. His conviction regarding the inevitability of a massively destructive conflagration was confirmed that very evening by a lavish military parade and raucous celebration, extending well into the night. Sherman took a jaundiced view of such events, characterizing them in his diary as benighted revelry in the face of impending downfall.

On February 24, 1861, Sherman went to the railroad station early and boarded the train that would carry him to the North. During the lengthy journey he noted the foment and the misguided sense of excitement that gripped the South, what Mark Twain would aptly christen "the Sir Walter Scott disease." This mercurial disease would overwhelm the temporarily irrational South—and in time leave it devastated. As the train drew closer to the North, the Southern aura of excitement was replaced by a general uncertainty of what was to come, for the North seemed calm and even placid in its ignorance of the implications of secession. This blasé attitude was in sharp contrast to Sherman—the tall, slender, blue-eyed passenger who stepped on the platform of every station stop to smoke his small cigars while nervously pacing until the whistle announced the train's impending departure. Sherman understood perhaps better than most what was coming. He left the South much like a brokenhearted suitor, only to return with a fierce and marauding army as its ruthless conqueror.

General Sherman and Party.

Portrait of "General Sherman and Party" taken in San Fransisco in 1876 - Mrs. Ellen Ewing Sherman, Senator Donald Cameron (Republican Leader of Pennsylvania), Minnie Chauteau (later Henshaw), General William Tecumseh Sherman, Eliza McCormack Cameron, Virginia Cameron, Ellie Sherman, Thomas Duffy (Democratic Leader of Pennsylvania), Lieutenant Francis Vinton Green, Thomas Ewing Sherman, James McCormack Cameron, and Philemon Tecumseh Sherman. A note on the reverse reads "this entire party made the trip through the west and to San Francisco with General Sherman in a 'Private' car."

The Sherman family posed on the porch of John Sherman's home in Mansfield, Ohio, circa 1886 - C. W. Molton, Fanny Molton, Elizabeth Reese, John Babcock, Cecelia Sherman Lampton, General William Tecumseh Sherman, Sarah Sherman, Hoyt Sherman, Ellen Ewing Sherman, Kate Willock, Mary McCallum Sherman, P. T. Sherman, Minnie Probasco Molton, Addie Wilong Sherman

Exterior view of a home built in 1859 by General
William Tecumseh Sherman in Indian Creek, Kansas.
The photo was taken October 22, 1891.

1888 Portrait of General William Tecumseh
Sherman in uniform as an older man

EIGHT

The Debacle at Bull Run

BEFORE SHERMAN SERVED as a colonel in the first great battle of the Civil War, he dabbled with many career options. Two things seem clear: First of all, he wanted a position that gave him financial security so that he could manage to keep his family close—and Ohio and the Ewings at a distance. Second, he hoped to resurrect his military career with a high rank upon being recommissioned. Sherman also sensed that the first wave of Union generals would not fare well, and this made him hold back from joining the ranks too quickly.

On his way north from Louisiana, he stopped in St. Louis to assess his employment possibilities. He consulted with his old army buddy and banking associate Henry Turner and tried to obtain a high-ranking position in the treasury department office in St. Louis. This denied him, he settled for the presidency of a trolley car company named the Fifth Street Railway. Sherman took on the trolley car job with full force and for the brief period during which he held the position he managed to save expenses by reducing the work force by a third. He also improved efficiency through his unstinting on-site supervision of the trolley cars and his insistence that they adhere to the company's operational timetables. Unfortunately, despite his practical successes within the company, he couldn't seem to make ends meet. He had brought his family out from Ohio and installed them in a rented house, the expenses of which overwhelmed his income and taxed his reserves, despite having sold some of Ellen's possessions. He was in his office when word arrived on April 13 that Fort Sumter had fallen, defeated by a Confederate militia under the command of his old superior officer, Robert Anderson, with whom Sherman was still friendly. This catastrophe triggered offers for Sherman to resume his military career. Instead of immediately jumping in to serve, he took his time and weighed his offers. His brother John believed Sherman could easily join the Ohio militia as a general, although Sherman held back, frustrating his brother in the process. As a professionally trained soldier, Sherman was wary of the great volume of volunteers and raw recruits being enlisted by the Union. He did not think the new Lincoln administration had any better idea of what lay in store for the country than had James Buchanan's outgoing administration. When Lincoln called for seventy-five thousand volunteers, Sherman felt confirmed in his skepticism, knowing the number was far too small. He believed the Union would need four times that many.

Furthermore, Sherman speculated that any army of citizen soldiers fielded by the Union would be little more than an unruly and anarchic mob. Having dealt with volunteers and raw recruits during his career as an officer, both in Florida and in California, Sherman held them in extremely low regard. Sherman was firmly convinced that because of the ineptitude of such troops the first Union generals to lead battles would suffer humiliation and consequently endure the embarrassment of being replaced. The realization of his military aspirations, nevertheless, proved irresistible. On May 8, William Tecumseh Sherman picked up a pen and wrote to Secretary of War Simon Cameron. The response was not long in coming. Only twelve days later he learned that he was to command one of many rapidly formed new regiments as a colonel. His appointment came through on June 6 and he quickly sublet the St. Louis house and left for Washington, dispatching Ellen and the children once again back to Lancaster.

The chaos and confusion of the Union at the inception of the Civil War have been well documented. When Sherman reached Washington, he found it in a state of uproar and aimless anticipation and his fears were confirmed. Given Sherman's personality, with its obsessive need for order, this state of affairs was anathema to him.

At that time General in Chief Winfield Scott still headed the army, but at seventy-five the aging hero was not up to his nickname of "Old Fuss and Feathers." Indeed, he was suffering from multiple infirmities, which prompted his detractors to dub him "Old Fat and Feeble." On November 1, he would be forced to resign as general in chief of the army by the ambitious field commander George B. McClellan, who conveniently had many supporters in Congress. But that summer, before Scott's overthrow, the old warrior remembered Sherman when the newly appointed colonel reported to him in his living room. Scott could barely manage a trip to his office, suffering as he was from obesity, rheumatism, dropsy, gout, and an assortment of other ailments and infirmities, but his mind was still sharp. Scott had full recall of his meeting with Sherman in New York nearly a dozen years earlier in January 1850. Now that the Civil War had broken out, Sherman most likely would have reminded his superior of the prediction he had made those many years ago. Though a Virginian and a graduate of William and Mary, Scott had remained loyal to the Union and had drawn up the Anaconda Plan for the defeat of the Confederacy. The strategy laid out in this plan was much discounted, even mocked early on, but years later it was implemented by Sherman with the help of Ulysses S. Grant. Soon thereafter, Scott invited Sherman to dinner and gave him his first assignment: to inspect the military installations and their garrisons in and around Washington. There was considerable fear that the Confederacy was going to invade the city, the presence of its threatening armies massed in northern Virginia being common knowledge. Sherman executed this job with his usual diligence, and completed it before June was out, when new orders came through for him. He was to take charge of Fort Corcoran, across the Potomac in northern Virginia, on the future site of the city of Alexandria. The fort housed five militia regiments, four from New York and one from Wisconsin. This was a daunting task. In letters to Ellen, Sherman complained of lack of sleep, so long and arduous were his days filled with the problems of an unprepared army. The troops were ostensibly seasoned infantrymen but they were not artillerymen. They did not know how to operate the large cannons placed in the fort under their charge. Adding to troubles, the Wisconsin regiment at Fort Corcoran wore gray uniforms barely distinguishable from the new uniforms of the Confederate troops. The fort was incomplete, and the troops were charged with its completion though they were unskilled at construction.

Such absurdities typified the early days of the war for the Union army and led to serious exasperation for Sherman. Adding to his burden, Congress began demanding an immediate attack on the nearby Confederate armies in northern Virginia. Winfield Scott opposed such action, believing correctly that the federal forces were not yet up to it. Further complicating this demand for immediate action was the restless and unruly state of the soldiers. Many had volunteered merely for the three-month tour of duty called for when President Lincoln initially exhorted them to active service. There were already serious grumblings among the soldiers indicating they were ready to return home and that if an attack was not launched soon, they would simply defect. It is easy to see the folly of the North in expecting this horrifying war to be over quickly. This matched the folly of the outgunned South in having similar expectations. Both thought the enemy would be crushed early and surrender quickly. Many on both sides expected America to become two nations—one a highly centralized federal union, and the other a loosely affiliated states' rights confederation. They were wrong.

When the war first broke out, Winfield Scott appointed Colonel Robert E. Lee to head the Union army. This arrangement lasted all of one day, until their mutual home state of Virginia seceded and Lee resigned and headed home. Scott then chose General Irvin McDowell for this important position. After three months of mounting pressure for action, Scott reluctantly told McDowell to initiate an attack. On July 16, McDowell moved his army deeper into Virginia. His ragtag army was anything but a trained and skilled fighting force. Sherman wrote the pro-verbial "farewell letter" to Ellen, in case he perished, and then set out with his five regiments to assist McDowell and the rest of the Union troops. The Union army was neither efficient nor professional, even in the basic task of marching. The greenhorn troops were silly and insubordinate and given to brigandage, stealing livestock and valuables from farms they passed, some set-ting fires as well. McDowell's army took two and a half days to cover roughly twenty miles. Along this erratic march troops and vehicles both lost their way, wasting valuable time. Because the standard army pace is three miles an hour, or a mile covered every twenty minutes, this distance should easily have been attained in a little more than eight hours. When ordered to increase their pace—or to do anything at all—the troops typically back-talked, jeered, or slowed down even more. Such behavior must only have reinforced Sherman's contempt for untrained volunteers and raw recruits. When on July 18 Sherman and his brigade had their first brush with the enemy, the colonel was not encouraged. He later wrote to Ellen that the volunteers chose to do pretty much as they pleased, even in combat, and would often fire their rifles on impulse, even when the enemy was clearly out of range. In addition, friendly fire was a great danger due to such lack of discipline.

Three days later, on July 21, the first large-scale battle of the Civil War broke out, known in the North as the Battle of Bull Run and in the South as the Battle of First Manassas. General P. G. T. Beauregard, who had won glory in the siege of Fort Sumter, led the main Confederate army. A second Confederate army under General Joseph E. Johnston, formerly stationed in the Shenandoah Valley, backed up Beauregard. The Union strategy devised by McDowell was basically sound: he would attack the Confederates head-on from the north, then he would send a large force around their lines to the east, with the objective of outflanking the Confederate right, thereby cutting off the Confederate rail lines that led to Richmond. When fierce hostilities broke out at first light, the execution of this plan did not materialize as envisioned by McDowell.

On both sides the troops were green, but in numbers the Confederates had a slight advantage. It's also safe to assume that the Southern troops were more highly motivated since they were fighting on their home territory, invaded and under siege, their backs to the wall. In addition, the Southerners had been agitated for fifteen years with the growing power of the federal government trying to impose its will; so warfare had begun to seem fairly inevitable, leading to extensive training and preparation.

Consequently the Southern troops were in most instances drawn from better-trained state militias. But even if not, they were often more easily converted into able soldiers since most of them had grown up in rural settings, where hunting and the use of sidearms and rifles was more common. The South also had a far more pronounced military tradition going for it. The North, on the other hand, had many troops from urban environments where hunting experience and the use of sidearms and rifles was far less common. Furthermore, the Southern troops had been enlisted for a year of service, four times longer than the ninety-day commitment of the Northern troops.

One other factor accounted for the differences between the Confederate and Union armies. The new president of the Confederacy, Jefferson Davis, was a West Point graduate who had served with distinction in the Mexican War, whereas Lincoln had no military experience at all to draw upon and relied completely on his generals for guidance and advice in all matters military. In contrast, Davis viewed himself as a colleague on equal footing with his generals and therefore endeavored more enthusiastically to supply their manpower and matériel needs. Davis's military knowledge and combat experience gave the South an edge at the beginning of the war. Davis eventually proved mettlesome and counterproductive in the eyes of his generals, though, viewing himself as a much more accomplished strategist than in fact he was. Due to ego, Davis, much like Hitler eighty years later, ultimately hindered his generals and hobbled them in their best efforts to prosecute the war effectively. Lincoln did the opposite: he remained aloof and went through generals until he found the two he really needed, Ulysses S. Grant and Grant's close friend William Tecumseh Sherman. Roughly put, Davis micromanaged and perished while Lincoln delegated and triumphed.

These developments, however, lay far in the future. On that

hot afternoon of July 21, Sherman's regiments were involved at the epicenter of battle, trying to dislodge the Confederate artillery and infantry from a knoll, called simply Henry House Hill. All afternoon the fighting for the hill was intense, with the Confederates pouring cannon and rifle fire down upon Union troops who were attempting to storm the hill and overrun their position. Sherman's five regiments all took a turn at rushing the Confederates but none met with success. Among the principal defenders of the hill was Confederate legend General Thomas "Stonewall" Jackson, the former artillery professor at VMI. Of course, as with much of the Civil War, there are differing opinions about what actually happened that day, but the consensus is that the Confederates repulsed the Federal forces after a pitched battle. The Union troops became disoriented, many panicked, and finally the entire force retreated in disorganized chaos.

For hours the conflict had been a stalemate until the Union troops abruptly fell apart, panicked, and took flight. Psychologically the defeat rocked the North. The sight of the vanquished Union troops and equipment returning to Washington across the Potomac was not reassuring to the residents of the capital, who, now more than ever, feared an invasion by enemy armies. A new reality sank in immediately: troops would be needed for much longer than ninety days. This war was not going to be a short conflict. Following the battle, Sherman was immediately cast into depression, realizing the utter weakness of his raw volunteer forces. Undertrained, unruly, uneducated, and insubordinate, his troops were a nightmare to command. He wrote a brief letter to Ellen, indicating the magnitude of the Union failure and feeling somewhat sorry for himself, as he was fearful his reputation and career would suffer.

In a week his view of the defeat had changed. General McDowell gave Sherman solid marks in his report on the battle, as did Sherman's immediate superior, General Daniel Tyler. This encouraged Sherman but did not change his pessimistic views of what the war would ultimately entail. Predictably, Sherman publicly denigrated the press for stooping to sensationalism. Just as predictably, he impugned the Northern politicians for their ignorance of the task now facing them, citing the recent resolve and might on the part of the Confederates as desperate concerns. He was highly unimpressed with Lincoln in particular. He wondered openly if a democracy could form an army of dedicated soldiers rather than a mob of insubordinate louts. His acute misanthropy and his elitist contempt for "commoners" surged to the fore. As he had most of his life, he believed only "aristocrats" of his own class were worthy of leadership roles. Sherman's performance at Bull Run had positioned him for a promotion to brigadier general, which came through shortly thereafter. His persistent skepticism combined with his caginess made him reluctant to accept a hasty elevation in command. He didn't want his record tarnished by Bull Run–like defeats caused by the poor quality of the troops he was commanding.

At first he was unaware, however, of one important fact about his new assignment: He would be heading west, and heading west always sounded good to Sherman.

NINE

Lost in the Wilderness

A FEW WEEKS after Bull Run, when the new promotions were posted, Sherman's name was at the top of the list of new brigadier generals: ahead of Ulysses S. Grant, Ambrose Burnside, and his old West Point sidekick George H. Thomas. Naturally Sherman's spirits rose. They became even more elevated when he was invited to a meeting at the White House with President Lincoln, General in Chief Winfield Scott, and other high-ranking officials to discuss the mutinies among Union troops, a crisis that had become epidemic. One of many major changes during the Civil War was the strong influence of media coverage. Photography came into its own and so did newspapers with their new up-close-and-personal chronicles of events in the field. Along with these innovations came the problem of indiscreet publishing. Papers would quietly obtain classified information and then eagerly publish it, compromising one army or the other in the process.

Usually it was the Union army that suffered, since the Southern press, speaking for a nation under siege, took a more cautious approach to what it published. In the North, the sensationalist press ran rampant, further inciting the public who already felt endangered and underprepared. Militia leaders and even the rank and file let loose their venom toward leadership, adding fuel to an already raging fire. Prominent newspapers published these disagreements without a hint of remorse, to titillate the public and increase sales.

During that summer of 1861, Robert Anderson, Sherman's former commander in Florida, sent word to Sherman to meet him at the Willard Hotel. When Sherman arrived, Anderson's position of influence was apparent. Sherman walked into a room full of powerful officials, including Andrew Johnson, future vice president under Lincoln. All in the room had something in common: they were all from the West, and they all had strong feelings toward keeping the West in the Union, specifically, the pivotal state of Kentucky. Both sides were eyeing many Southern and swing states, but Kentucky was obviously of crucial military importance because of its border.

Both the borders with Ohio and Indiana were defined by the Ohio River, which offered a nearly perfect defensive landscape. With terrain full of natural redoubts and sizable hills rising on the Kentucky side in many sections, the Union generals were eager to secure it for the North. For the very same reasons the Confederate generals coveted control. Kentucky had advocates within it for both sides. During the summer and fall months of 1861, the North and the South each seized sections of the state and vague battle lines were drawn. Robert Anderson had seemed a perfect choice to head up the Northern effort, as a native of Kentucky as well as a hero of the battle for Fort Sumter. He had been granted clearance to select three brigadier generals to aid him in his effort. He had summoned Sherman to the brainstorming session at the Willard Hotel to inform him that he was one of the three. As for the other two, Sherman was pleased to be working alongside his old friend George H. Thomas, as well as Ambrose Burnside. At the hotel meeting, Anderson told Sherman that he wanted him to be his second-in-command. Sherman was pleased to hear this. He had always liked Anderson, and he had always been attracted to the West. He had one condition that he immediately made known and then expressed later during a meeting with President Lincoln. Sherman specified that he would serve as Anderson's number two provided he would never be raised to number one. With his celebrated sense of humor, Lincoln found Sherman's humility refreshing and made a joke to the effect that he didn't have enough command positions to go around among his generals anyway. Sherman was neither humble nor joking, but simply calculating. He wanted to avoid being in charge of untrained and unprofessional troops that he felt would embarrass him. Egotistical and narcissistic as ever, Sherman was seeking to preserve his chance at military fame. Ever since the days of West Point, Sherman had been conscious of the way he might appear to historians, knowing his experiences in Florida and California had done nothing to preserve his memory. He did not want to take the lead in a questionable project and thus further taint his reputation.

Even though the Kentucky state legislature—in the days following the attack on Fort Sumter and the secession of various nearby states—had declared Kentucky "neutral," Kentucky could not remain so. Both North and South ignored this declaration of neutrality and moved military units into the strategic state. In early September, when Confederate troops under General Gideon Pillow seized the important city of Columbia, Union troops under the always decisive Ulysses S. Grant retaliated by taking over Paducah, yet another important city. Both in western Kentucky, these cities were crucial to control of the river routes that merged nearby. In the northwestern part of the state, the Tennessee River flowed into the Ohio at Paducah, and then, shortly thereafter, the Ohio itself, flowing to the southwest, merged with the Mississippi. In the southwestern part of the state, the Mississippi flowed past Columbia on its way to St. Louis and points south until it disappeared into the Gulf of Mexico south of New Orleans.

As Winfield Scott's Anaconda Plan had made clear, control of the Mississippi river traffic was key to controlling the West. The South could be isolated in the tightening of a snakelike noose. This encirclement by ground forces would thus be augmented, on the Gulf of Mexico and on the Atlantic seaboard, by an effective naval blockade, shutting down the South's seaports, while controlling its principal inland waterway, the mighty Mississippi. Like Winfield Scott, Sherman and Grant recognized the importance of controlling the Mississippi right from the start of the conflict.

Anderson recognized the importance of controlling the Mississippi, too, but he recognized as well the importance of that monumental nineteenth-century invention, the railroad. The railroad was another feature of modern warfare the Civil War would bring to the forefront as no other military conflict had. After assigning Sherman to tour the capitals of the states surrounding Kentucky to assess their moods and appraise their resources, Anderson ordered him to form a fighting unit and defend the lines of the important Louisville and Nashville Railroad. This line ran down the center of the state from Louisville before dog-legging southwest at Bowling Green, after which it continued south and slightly west to cross the state line with Tennessee before reaching Nashville. Control of this rail artery would be of the utmost importance and would require Sherman to control important sections of the rail line concentrated around a place called Muldraugh's Hill.

While Sherman set about the task of achieving this strategic defense, he was tormented with angst, much as he had been during the situation with the Committee of Vigilance crisis in San Francisco when he was head of the state militia. In that instance, he had summarily resigned as head of the state militia and suffered public humiliation as a result. Now, with a fearful war upon him, his fears mounted and threatened to run away with him. He thought his defensive positions around Muldraugh's Hill were inadequate. Rumors that a large Confederate force was massing just south of his position preyed on his composure. His worries grew. Reports circulated that a substantial unit of Confederate cavalry lurked a mere fifty miles away. Surely this unit could strike

quickly and chew up Sherman's supply line as well as his telegraph communications back to headquarters. Sherman's fearful
imaginings were in vain, though. The Confederates were equally
convinced that their forces were outmanned and outgunned.
Consequentially they set about a campaign of rapid movement to
simulate a much larger force in play.

This strategy worked, largely because it played more on
Sherman's imagination than his reason. He saw himself and his
men imperiled in the midst of hostile territory. He was convinced
that most of the locals were spying and reporting back to the
Confederates, massed only miles to the south, within quick striking distance. While his imagination and fear ran away with him,
Sherman received an order from Anderson to return immediately to
Louisville to meet with him. He later claimed that he knew from the
tone of Anderson's summons that he was resigning his post, which
was indeed the case. What's more, despite Sherman's attempts
to prevent just such an event, Anderson had recommended he
assume command of the Department of the Cumberland. This, to
Sherman's intense displeasure, came to pass. When it did, Sherman
began to write everyone he could, including Lincoln and Secretary
of the Treasury Salmon Chase, to emphasize the vulnerability of
his army's position. He and his men needed reinforcements, they
needed supplies, they needed equipment—in short, they needed
everything. Secretary Chase wrote back assurances that Sherman
would receive the needed supplies and counseled Sherman not to
overestimate the might of the opposing forces and not to abandon
plans of aggressive movements against these forces. Chase was
attempting to buck Sherman up, but the attempt failed.

After being in charge for little more than a week, on October 17 Sherman visited Secretary of War Simon Cameron as he passed through Louisville on his way back to Washington. Cameron was accompanied by members of the press, as well as by Adjutant General Lorenzo Thomas. They all met in Sherman's ground floor room in Galt House, where Sherman then requested a private meeting with Cameron. This request was refused. Cameron explained that everyone in his party was a friend and that Sherman could speak freely among them. Not liking this arrangement, Sherman proceeded to rise and lock the hotel room door. Then he poured forth a litany of concern and woe in an intensely excited manner. In spite of this behavior, Cameron took him seriously and diverted troops destined for Missouri to reinforce Sherman in Kentucky. The secretary also indicated that more personnel support and supplies of maté-riel would be arriving rapidly. Despite this, Sherman told the secretary that in order to defend Kentucky properly, he would require sixty thousand men. What was more, to go on the offensive in Kentucky, Sherman would require a force two hundred thousand strong. At this pronouncement, Cameron erupted in astonishment and asked in a loud voice where all these troops were to come from. Sherman responded that the North could muster all the men necessary. After Cameron left Louisville he traveled to Lexington where other Kentuckians drew a similarly dire picture of the gathering Confederate forces to the south. As for Sherman back in Louisville, his mind continued to race with negative scenarios. He confided in a letter to Ellen that he was outnumbered three to one. In the blink of an eye he revised this estimate in a letter to his brother John, telling him he was actually outnumbered five to one.

On October 30, thirteen days after the meeting with Cameron, the *New York Tribune* reporter who had been present at the hotel meeting in Sherman's room published a highly unflattering article, mocking Sherman's troop requests. He went further, depicting Sherman's manner and comportment as unseemly and unprofessional, especially his paranoid treatment of members of the press. Two days later in Washington, McClellan's maneuvers against Winfield Scott bore results as the old general was displaced. McClellan wrote immediately to Sherman that he wanted regular reports from him on conditions in Kentucky. Sherman responded with a barrage of increasingly dire and alarming dispatches before requesting to be relieved of command in Kentucky and returned to his old post at the head of his former brigade. Concerned by the tone and tenor of these communiqués, McClellan sent his aide, Colonel Thomas M. Key, to Kentucky to visit with Sherman. After several days in Sherman's company, Key reported to McClellan that he thought Sherman was on the brink of a nervous collapse. When other high-ranking officials, including Senator Andrew Johnson, confirmed Sherman's condition, McClellan replaced him with General Don Carlos Buell on November 13.

Sherman's eccentric behavior had drawn much comment and notice. He had disdained sleep, staying up each night until 3:00 a.m. to check for telegrams. When the telegraph office closed briefly for the night, Sherman paced the hotel corridor outside of his room, puffing on endless cigars, worrying intensely.

McClellan issued new orders for Sherman, sending him to serve under his old friend from California, General Henry W. Halleck, whose headquarters was located in St. Louis.

When Sherman arrived in St. Louis, his condition concerned Halleck, who nevertheless assigned him to inspect some troop positions, a routine and fairly easy task. Sherman set about the inspection but soon urged Halleck to consolidate the scattered Union forces lest they be overrun by Confederate troops. This was a sound military assessment that Halleck shortly thereafter implemented, though Sherman's charged and agitated condition in delivering this analysis so alarmed his friend that Halleck had an army doctor evaluate Sherman. The doctor pronounced Sherman in too high a state of agitation for command and recommended an extended rest. Meanwhile, Sherman's letters home had upset Ellen deeply. They reflected his massive remorse and depression from resigning his command in Kentucky. He had proved himself to be a total failure yet again and as a result was entertaining thoughts of suicide, which he wrote about in detail to Ellen. He confided in her that the only thing stopping him was thinking of her and the children. Alarmed, Ellen contacted Sherman's brother John, to whom Sherman had also confided his suicidal thoughts, and together they traveled to St. Louis. They returned Sherman to Lancaster for an urgently needed period of rest and recuperation. From the start of this episode, Ellen publicly stuck by her husband, insisting that nothing much had gone awry. Yet clearly Brigadier General Sherman had suffered a mild manic phase, what is commonly called a nervous breakdown. Now he was retreating to the care of the

Ewings, to place himself under the wing of his powerful father-in-law, with his apparently inexhaustible connections. And once again, Ewing's benevolence would prove the pivot to destiny in Sherman's life.

TEN

Redemption at Shiloh

FOR ALL OF William Tecumseh Sherman's accomplishment, we must not underestimate the influence of the woman behind the scenes, Ellen Ewing Sherman. By the end of 1861, her wounded husband was headed for a life of embarrassment. The press had given him rough treatment—newspaper articles had described him as a "mad freak" and "insane," referring to his frenzied behavior in Kentucky, along with his precipitous decision to quit and look for a "quiet corner." But it was Ellen who set about immediately on a fierce and effective campaign of public relations "damage control," something her husband was unable to do in his state. First, she mobilized her influential father to pull every political string he could in Washington. This included enlisting President Lincoln in the cause of resurrecting Sherman's badly stained image.

Ellen insisted that Sherman's public humiliation must not be allowed and that it could not possibly be the final word. She eventually wrote to Lincoln, appealing to him on the grounds that the press and its nefarious reporters had slandered her talented and brave husband. She further informed the president that there were enemies lined up against her husband in a conspiracy to ruin him, fueled by jealousy and ambition. The wise and exceptionally diplomatic Lincoln, also having allegedly suffered through mental anguish, handled Ellen's contentions with compassion and sensitivity.

Tom Ewing was equally determined to help his son-in-law, as was Sherman's brother John. Their powers combined, the Ewing influence soon bore fruit. Ellen joined her father in the capital in late January and met face-to-face with the president at the White House. Adding to Sherman's brightening fate, Secretary of War Simon Cameron had been forced out for corruption. His replacement, Edwin M. Stanton, had long been friends with Tom Ewing. Things were moving in an optimistic, if familiar, direction. While Ellen, her father, and her brother-in-law were sounding out political connections in Washington, Sherman bounced back a bit in Lancaster and determined that his best chance to salvage his military career would be to lay low. He set upon abandoning his higher ambitions and offered himself for humbler service to his old friend General Halleck, whose career had been mercurial. After General Halleck cleaned up Missouri in relief of Fremont and placed it securely within the Union, he was elevated to command of what was then called the Department of the Mississippi. This was really the expanded

Department of the Missouri but newly inclusive of the Deep South states. As such, Halleck was based out of the capital as the overall commander of all Union forces in the West, including Missouri, Tennessee, and Mississippi. Ever mindful of the political influence of Sherman's family, Halleck took a prudent course. He was not nicknamed "Old Brains" for nothing. He posted Sherman to a training facility outside St. Louis called Benton Barracks as leader in charge. Halleck believed this posting was a low stress assignment that Sherman could handle without danger of relapse. Sherman was glad to have the role and he had rebounded sufficiently to perform his duties, but he did cling to the base at Benton Barracks without venturing outside, despite having many friends in St. Louis who wanted to see him. His reclusive tendencies were such that when his old comrade Henry Turner came to call on him, Sherman could not bring himself to go out to the gate to usher him in, which forced Turner to leave.

Wallowing in self-pity, Sherman speculated in a letter to Ellen that this behavior would likely prompt Turner to drop him. In addition to these problems, Sherman was still concerned about his misadventures at the outset of the war. He speculated that the congressional committee formed with the purpose of investigating the failed Battle of Bull Run would discover something Sherman had conveniently omitted from his report—that at one point in the heat of the battle he had become separated from his troops. Halleck had promised Sherman that he would place him again in charge of troops in the field when the time was right. Ever aware of Tom Ewing and his influence in Washington, Halleck kept his word, but only after Sherman had served effectively for a few months at Benton Barracks.

Meanwhile, things had gone well for the Union in Kentucky during the first two months of 1862. First, General George H. Thomas had led a Union victory at the Battle of Mill Springs on January 19. This triumph gave the Union forces control of the Cumberland Gap. The vanquished Confederates, whose leader, General Felix Zollicoffer, had been killed in the battle, left Kentucky altogether and withdrew to Tennessee. Two weeks later, on February 2, General Grant and his troops attacked the Confederates at Forts Henry and Donelson. These key forts commanded the Tennessee and the Cumberland Rivers at points where the rivers were separated by only a dozen miles, and also at points not far north of the Kentucky-Tennessee state line.

Grant distinguished himself with these two victories. Attacking aggressively with infantry supported by gunboats, Grant set the stage for his later important victories farther down the Mississippi Valley. Fort Henry fell on February 6 and Donelson fell on February 16. As overall commander for these victories, Halleck, always ambitious and political, was well pleased with the kudos he received in Washington. When plans called for assaults farther into the South, Halleck countered General in Chief McClellan's suggestion to appoint General Buell as leader of the first assault up the Cumberland River and went to bat for Sherman, vouching for his soundness of mind and his competence as a leader. McClellan agreed to Halleck's suggestion, though a doubtful Secretary of War Stanton requisitioned

reports and letters written by Sherman from Kentucky the previous fall. After reading them, he passed them along to Lincoln
after attaching a note recommending that Sherman *not* be given
this command in light of his erratic behavior in Kentucky. At first
Halleck was going to appoint General Charles F. Smith to lead
the initial Tennessee River expedition into the South. On merit,
this prominent leadership assignment should have gone to Grant.
Not surprisingly, given Grant's personality, he had been remiss in
filing his paperwork, which vexed the persnickety Halleck, who
consequently penciled in Smith for the assignment. Meanwhile,
Halleck had posted Sherman to Paducah to supervise a staging
area and river traffic.

As usual, Sherman was assiduous and effective with these
administrative tasks. At the same time, he was diligent in executing a task closer to his heart: assembling the division Halleck had
assured him he could take into the field as commander. In short
order this indeed came about, and Halleck directed Sherman
to load his men into steamers and proceed up the Tennessee
River to Fort Henry and there link up with General Smith and
his other three divisions. The objective now was for Smith to
take his incursion force up the river to Corinth, a crucial railroad
junction where a main east-west line crossed a main north-south
line. The Memphis and Charleston Railroad also had its repair
shops nearby in Burnsville, Mississippi, and, moreover, well outside Corinth there was an important railroad bridge over Bear
Creek. Sherman made clear to his subordinates that the object
was to break the enemy communications system, not to engage in
any large-scale fighting. Nothing went right because, as so often

happened in the course of the Civil War, inclement weather intervened. Torrential rains poured down and the Tennessee River rose ominously, sometimes as quickly as half a foot an hour, flooding fields and plains and turning roads into quagmires. As a result, Sherman had no choice but to abort the initial foray. As soon as the weather relented, Sherman made adjustments and tried again, but he was under observation from Confederate pickets, forcing him to operate under the cover of night. The rains returned and continued, however, and conditions forced Sherman to abandon even his minimum objective of knocking out the most essential rail and telegraph lines.

Clearly, he was overambitious operating under such adverse conditions, likely overcompensating for the criticism heaped upon him the previous fall and overdetermined to prove his worthiness for command in active combat. He nonetheless fell back with his troops on March 16 to a spot large enough to accommodate his force as well as other divisions on the west bank of the Tennessee River. This was Pittsburg Landing, twenty miles from Corinth. Other divisions soon joined Sherman's troops. Grant by now had been given charge of the expedition, since Smith had sustained an injury that had become infected. Following behind Sherman and his unit, a day later, on March 17, Grant set up headquarters at Savannah, Tennessee, a few miles north of Pittsburg Landing. All told, between the troops under Grant at Savannah and the troops that had joined Sherman's unit at Pittsburg Landing, the Union forces totaled forty thousand. In addition, General Buell was on his way south with another twenty thousand troops. Halleck planned to assume field command of the entire Union force as soon as Grant and Buell linked up.

Unknown to either Grant or Sherman, as the press would soon report, Confederate general Albert Sidney Johnston had assembled a large army in Corinth and on its outskirts. General Beauregard, the Confederate hero of Fort Sumter who had also acquitted himself so ably in routing the Union at Bull Run, strengthened Johnston personally as well as militarily. Johnston's recent losses in Tennessee had drawn copious red-toothed criticism in the Southern press, with accusations that he was an incompetent drunk who should be relieved of command by Jefferson Davis. Davis, however, flatly refused to do so, extolling instead Johnston's great credits as a combat-hardened general's general. Regardless, Johnston was downcast from all the negative coverage and the attempted ouster, so Beauregard's positive energy and attitude were most welcome to him.

Some fifteen thousand of the troops assembled under Johnston had been brought north from New Orleans under the command of another old friend of Sherman's, General Braxton Bragg. The Confederates were formidable and ready, and had at their disposal that priceless asset in warfare, the element of surprise. Most of the criticism later heaped on Grant and Sherman in hindsight for not detecting the large Confederate army forming under their noses was highly justified. It was an entire three weeks from the time Sherman moved his troops into bivouac at Pittsburg Landing until the Confederates attacked; and for Grant and his contingent settling in a few miles distant at Savannah, the interlude was one day shorter. There was no excuse for intelligence officers and rangers failing to detect the enemy. It is possible, however, that Sherman *did* know of the gathering storm.

Perhaps Sherman was too committed to showing himself courageous to have signaled fear in the face of amassing Confederate troops. He may have known that his back was to the wall as a field commander. He would either have to come through here, on the battlefield, or he would have to try to salvage his military career as a behind-the-lines quartermaster. This he had already determined a few months earlier during his days of recovery in Lancaster.

Grant was Grant: unflappable, a leader not given to excessive worry or to an overactive imagination, and a fighter buttressed to the eyeballs with confidence. No matter the ferocity of the battle or the combat prowess of the enemy, he and his troops would prevail. Endeared by Grant's spirit, Sherman had already started to hold his new commander in high esteem, impressed as he was by the confidence and boldness with which Grant had conquered both Forts Henry and Donelson. The Union troops gathered at Pittsburg Landing were untested, undertrained, and inexperienced, all of which nearly drove Sherman to extremes of exasperation. They would wander off, give discipline a wide berth, and show an extreme aversion to rationale. In the wet conditions resulting from the heavy rainfall, they continued to fire their weapons, testing that their powder was sufficiently dry, and at the same time alerting enemy pickets and scouts to their position. In his ire following general inspections, Sherman imposed fines on these troops for spent cartridges, but this had little effect.

Fortunately for the Union commanders, the Confederate officers faced many of the same problems. Vast numbers of their troops were recent recruits and volunteers, with the same deficiencies and amateur qualities as the Union troops. War is often chaos, disorganization, and confusion even when the battle is waged between experienced soldiers. The newly gathered Confederate army made a hash of traversing the twenty-two miles from Corinth to Pittsburg Landing once they finally moved up and positioned themselves for an attack. In fact, the attack nearly didn't occur at all after Beauregard advised Johnston that, given the intelligence that Buell was on his way with reinforcements, the Confederates should withdraw to fight another day.

Beauregard argued further that since the Confederates had taken fully twice as long as they should have to move into an attack position, they had forfeited the element of surprise. This, he went on to say, had given Buell precious time to reach the Union lines and increase the Union advantage in both manpower and firepower.

Johnston was having none of this. Ready to attack, Johnston delivered a stirring speech to his assembled troops, which had quite the galvanizing effect. At daybreak on Sunday morning April 6, Johnston's troops fought savagely and initially pushed back the broad front of the Union lines at Pittsburg Landing. This attack along a broad front, against fixed positions, was Napoleonic. The objective Johnston sought was to break through the left flank of the Union lines and then roll the entire Union front to its right, in the direction of the mushy swamps and creeks bordering Pittsburg Landing to the north and the east.

By doing this, the Confederates would pin the Union troops in muddy terrain with the Tennessee River bank behind them, hardly a good way of escape for so large a number of troops if forced to retreat. Though brilliant in conception, this strategy was executed less-than-perfectly. The Confederates were old-fashioned and foolish. Instead of the broad frontal attack Johnston used, a wiser choice would have been to implement diversionary attacks on the center and on the right flank of the Union front, concentrating a breakthrough assault on the Union left flank. The Union left flank fought magnificently under General Benjamin Prentiss, one of whose officers had ignored Sherman's dismissal of a Confederate buildup and aptly investigated. This Union contingent engaged the advancing Confederate troops, buying precious preparation time for the rest of the troops back at Pittsburg Landing who were awakened by the burst of rifle and cannon fire. Prentiss and his men further distinguished themselves by falling back into a natural redoubt formed by a sunken road behind the Union left flank. This obstruction would earn the name the "Hornets' Nest" and would sustain for hours through attack after attack.

In spite of an all-out Confederate assault, the Union held the Hornets' Nest until late in the afternoon, when no option was left except surrender. Indeed, the Union lines had fallen back around the redoubt and left it surrounded by Confederate forces. At this point, the Confederates were doubly foolish in not concentrating their attack against the Union left flank rather than spreading their resources in a broad frontal assault. In addition, they chose not to bypass the Hornets' Nest and isolate it sooner, enabling them to pass beyond it to press their attack deeper into the Union lines.

Had the Southerners not made these two tactical mistakes, their objective might well have been attained. It's not inconceivable that they could have forced the Union troops to retreat, backing them up against the Tennessee River. As it was, the frustrated Johnston, in his determination to break through and roll up the Union left flank, rode forward to the front. There, while rallying his troops attacking the Union left flank, Johnston sustained a hit from a Union rifled musket. The bullet tore into his leg and severed an artery. He bled out rapidly and died on the spot.

Beauregard stepped into the breach and assumed sole command of the Confederate attack. About an hour before twilight, he made a decision still excoriated in the South: with time left to make one final assault, Beauregard disastrously chose instead to hold his position and resume the attack in the morning. Had he pressed one more concerted attack against the Union lines, with the left flank more vulnerable now that the Hornets' Nest had surrendered, the ultimate Southern objective might have been realized. The Union left flank may have crumbled, taking their center and right flanks back to a vulnerable position.

As it was, the Union forces, though pushed back, were able to retrench. The Union center and right flank held their own, although they did give considerable ground. Sherman gave an exceptional performance, scrambling everywhere, directing the fight with vigor and valor. He and Prentiss emerged as Union heroes for preventing a rout and another panicked retreat *a la* Bull Run. For his pains Sherman sustained a bullet wound in his right hand, a shoulder injury, and a close call when another bullet whistled through his hat, narrowly missing his head.

Accounts vary. Some say Sherman had three horses shot out from under him, others hold that it was actually four horses. The official record is that the federal government reimbursed Sherman for two mounts—half a dozen years later in 1868. Whatever the actual count, Sherman, covered with dirt, dust, and blood, his hand wrapped in a bloodstained handkerchief, was cheered heartily by his men. Always a man haunted by insecurity and determined to prove himself rather than simply *be* himself, that day Sherman had found his nerve and his métier.

Earlier that morning while having breakfast, Grant heard the guns and knew instantly a large-scale battle had erupted. He then scrambled forward nine miles from Savannah and arrived on the battle scene at Pittsburg Landing around midmorning. Like Sherman, he stayed busy all day directing the Union defense, moving behind the lines and acquitting himself well. Later that night, when Sherman spoke to Grant beneath a tree as they sheltered themselves from the rain, a disheveled Grant cupping his cigar to keep it dry, the equally disheveled Sherman remarked that the day had been savagely difficult for the Union troops.

Many of them had deserted and congregated beneath the bluffs of the Tennessee River bank. The following day might be a reprise, another ordeal. But in fact, many of the Confederate troops had also panicked under fire and fled. Stephen Crane's *Red Badge of Courage* is a representative Civil War novel that focuses on that aspect. The novel's hero panics under fire in his first battle, only to overcome his fear and fight gallantly in subsequent battles. Many combatants on both sides "saw the elephant" during that battle for the first time, a Civil War expression referring to the experience of being under fire in active combat.

Considering how badly things had gone for the North that day, Sherman was about to ask Grant what plans he had made for a retreat, when suddenly something held him back. Grant continued, responding to Sherman's original observation about the possibility of another fierce beating like the one that had caused the Federals to lose so much ground. Looking straight at Sherman from under the brim of his dripping hat, Grant calmly told him that the next day the Union troops would attack the Confederate troops and "lick 'em." Later that same night, when some of Grant's officers advised him to retreat in the morning, he was once again unemotional, calm, and consistent, countering that he intended instead to attack at daybreak. Grant correctly assessed the situation, realizing that he had 25,000 fresh troops to complement the 15,000 who had fought that day, and would be able to do so again next day: this gave the Union a total of 40,000 against the Confederate force that Grant, again correctly, surmised would have been reduced from its full strength down to about 20,000. Grant could see that more than 10,000 men lay wounded, many critically, on the field of battle. He knew that desertion on the Confederate side would have reduced their forces significantly as well.

A third factor also favored Grant's determination to attack. With the arrival of Buell and his regiments, the Union advantage in artillery had been increased and was further enhanced by the two Union gunboats in the Tennessee River. These boats featured eight-inch guns, which were enormous for that era. To Grant's way of thinking, the fact that retreat had even been suggested was preposterous and the advantage had clearly shifted to him. Ironically, Beauregard, on the other side, was prematurely congratulating himself, convinced that all he and his troops needed to do was mop up. Beauregard was so confident the Confederates had secured a monumental victory that he dispatched word to that effect to Jefferson Davis in Richmond before going to sleep comfortably in his friend Sherman's field command tent, abandoned in retreat near Shiloh Church.

Earlier, Beauregard had received a false report that Buell and his contingent had diverted their path to northern Alabama. The infamous Confederate leader of cavalry, Nathan Bedford Forrest, knew better. His scouts had watched through the night as Buell and his men disembarked from ferryboats to join Grant on the battlefield at Pittsburg Landing. Forrest frantically tried to alert Beauregard but failed to find him. He found instead other Confederate generals who did not take this intelligence seriously, dismissing it wholesale. Disgusted, Forrest gave up, announcing to these disbelieving generals that in the morning, "We'll be whipped."

While Beauregard and Bragg slept comfortably in Sherman's tent next to the Shiloh Methodist Meeting House, Grant declined his cozy cabin on a steamboat docked in the Tennessee River. He and Sherman both spent the night instead on the field with the troops, making sure that at dawn they were ready to attack. They did just that and within a few hours pushed the Confederate forces back to their original position from the previous day. Not only were the Southern troops under sharp attack and losing ground rapidly, but they also were psychologically shocked, realizing that their supposed victory had been illusory. By midafternoon Beauregard had no choice but to heed the advice of his adjutants and withdraw with his beaten army. He promptly issued the order to retreat. It had rained hard yet again, and the roads were an ugly mass of deep mud, rendering pursuit by the Union forces almost impossible. This was just as well. The Union troops were exhausted, many of them simply flopping down on the wet field to rest and sleep, despite the muddy mutilated bodies strewn all around them.

Sherman had acquitted himself brilliantly once more during that second day of fighting. The next morning he mustered two brigades to pursue the retreating Confederates a few miles down the road to Corinth. The only result, however, was a brief firefight with Forrest's cavalry, who were protecting the Southern rear. Forrest was wounded during this skirmish, which served to frustrate him even further and pretty much put the exclamation point on the Southern defeat. Halleck arrived and assumed overall command of the Union army from Grant. General Pope's recently formed Army of the Mississippi had joined, increasing the force to one hundred thousand men strong. This huge army finally marched for Corinth, the crucial Confederate railway junction. A man of great caution, Halleck had his entire army entrench itself at the outbreak of even the smallest skirmish, despite his advantages in manpower and firepower. "Old Brains" had a tendency to do everything by the book, and as a result, the Union advantage was lost, a mistake Grant would not have made. Demoted by Halleck to second in command, a disenchanted Grant requested a transfer. Meanwhile, desperate to retain Corinth, Beauregard called in troops from all over the South. In the space of a few weeks he had assembled a force seventy thousand strong, including veterans of Shiloh who had since recovered. Because of an inadequate water supply, however, and the overcrowding of troops, Corinth had become something of a health liability. The waste and refuse from the troops befouled what little water supply there was and literally thousands succumbed to typhoid and to dysentery, while the wounded perished from infection.

This same fate befell Union general Smith, Sherman's former superior whose precombat injury to his leg had made possible Sherman's ascendancy to command at Shiloh. Back in Savannah, the site of Grant's old headquarters, Smith died of infection in bed in his hotel room, yet another indirect casualty of that great encounter. Because Corinth had by now become something of a cesspool and because Halleck, slow but steady, had managed to surround the town and bring in his big cannons, Beauregard underwent a change of heart and mind. On May 25 he retreated, having reevaluated the importance of Corinth as a rail junction. This he did with great aplomb and secrecy.

His entire army, save for a few stragglers and wounded left behind at Corinth, proceeded fifty miles south to Tupelo, Mississippi, where Beauregard bivouacked and declared this strategic retreat "the equivalent of a great victory." Jefferson Davis, however, disagreed. When Beauregard took a unilateral leave of absence to collect himself and regain his health, Jefferson quickly replaced him with Braxton Bragg, knowing that another such "victory" would be nothing less than the undoing of the South.

Shiloh is a biblical term that means "place of peace," proving once again that history has a perverse sense of humor and a stout appetite for irony. When Sherman chose Shiloh Methodist Meeting House for his headquarters a few days before the battle, he had no idea the name Shiloh would become so famous—or infamous, if one's allegiance lay below the Mason-Dixon Line— or that the site would play host to the greatest battle waged on the North American continent up until then. More than 100,000 men—60,000 Federals and 40,000 Confederates—had fought fiercely for two days straight. The dead, the dying, the grievously injured, and the permanently disfigured all lay about the blood-soaked field of battle. Before the first shot was fired, Sherman, like many others, had perhaps noted the peaceful little pond in the middle of the field and the peach blossom orchard in full bloom just beyond the left flank of the Union front line. The idyllic pond would come to be known henceforth as "Bloody Pond," because so many wounded and dying soldiers would hurl themselves into the waters of the pond, seeking relief from their pain. The peaceful, bucolic peach orchard, blooming healthily in the throes of early spring, was also the death site of Confederate general Albert Sidney Johnston, shot dead almost instantly astride his charger. After those two fateful days, the charming little church made of crude logs, the tranquil pond, and the flowering peach orchard would all pass into American lore.

So, too, would Sherman's resurrected career and his enduring image. A man encumbered with disgrace, he emerged from Shiloh a man covered in glory, despite early claims by the Northern press of his and Grant's lack of preparedness. When Grant and Sherman were first criticized, Grant, typically, said nothing. Sherman, on the other hand, foolishly embroiled himself in protracted public exchanges with his critics, including one with the lieutenant governor of Ohio. Sherman did not remove himself from that argument until ordered by Halleck to desist.

Seemingly incapable of withstanding any criticism without flaring back at his detractors, Sherman maintained perpetual spats with various newspapers throughout his career. He continually proved he was simply too thin-skinned and too insecure to ignore his critics and enemies. Grant, in contrast, continued his lifelong habit of doing the exact opposite, despite much greater provocation, especially when he later sat in the White House.

President Lincoln did not yet know it, but Shiloh had been the audition for the team of generals who would secure victory over the Confederacy.

As we know, Grant and Sherman prosecuted the remainder of the Union war effort with savage efficiency. Relentless and unflinching, Grant pressed onward, practicing all-out war, a new kind of war, not the Napoleonic warfare taught at West Point from the textbooks of Baron Jomini. Sherman did likewise, adding even speedier features to Grant's strategy of constant forward aggression. Sherman, however, despite the unprecedented mobility he brought to modern warfare, would cross a line, becoming almost feral as he implemented "total war" and all its gratuitous horrors. Shiloh set the pattern for how the remainder of the Civil War would play out. Through superior manpower, firepower, financial resources, matériel, and equipment, the industrial North waged a war of attrition on the agrarian South that ultimately wore it out. Yet such was the Southern grit and resolve that it would take another three years of unimaginable bloodletting and incalculable destruction before this ghastly victory was achieved. Sherman's prophecies once again would form into reality.

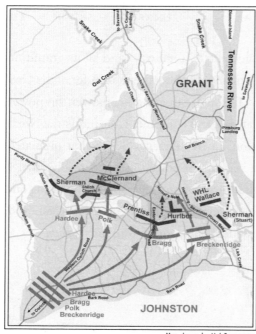

Troop movements in Shiloh the morning of April 6, 1865.

Map drawn by Hal Jespersen.

This graphic depiction shows Confederate strategy for the Battle of Shiloh.

Courtesy of the National Park Service, Historic Handbook Series No. 10

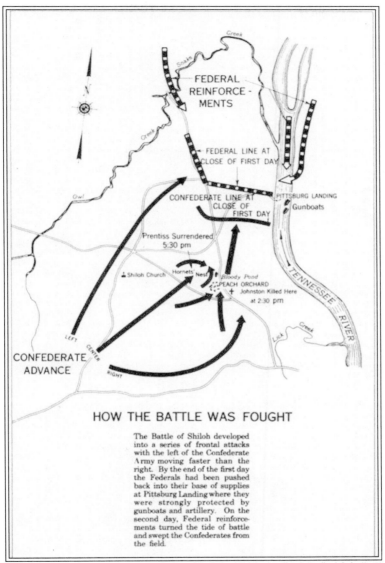

HOW THE BATTLE WAS FOUGHT

The Battle of Shiloh developed into a series of frontal attacks with the left of the Confederate Army moving faster than the right. By the end of the first day the Federals had been pushed back into their base of supplies at Pittsburg Landing where they were strongly protected by gunboats and artillery. On the second day, Federal reinforcements turned the tide of battle and swept the Confederates from the field.

Shiloh: How the Battle Was Fought – This rendering shows how the battle of Shiloh was fought.

ELEVEN

The Formative Interlude

DURING THE NEXT eighteen months, Sherman remained relatively composed and effective. During this period he suffered no mental distress on the scale of the mental and emotional collapse he endured in Kentucky in the autumn of 1861. Sherman undertook three assignments, two of which secured Grant's respect. Sherman was found lacking on the last of the three missions, which both disappointed Grant and compromised the Union mission. But concerning the first two assignments—the governance of occupied Memphis, followed by the siege of Vicksburg—Sherman was up to the mark and discharged his responsibilities well. Despite early criticism that Grant and Sherman were negligent in their positioning on Pittsburg Landing for a major battle like Shiloh, both generals emerged with enhanced careers as a result of their triumph. After General Halleck took Corinth, Sherman and his troops spent a short time repairing rail lines in Mississippi before moving on in high summer of 1862 to Memphis, where they encamped. As military governor of the city, Sherman set up headquarters in the Gayoso Hotel.

Sherman was fairly effective as an administrator, but not nearly so effective as he presumed. This self-congratulatory habit would reappear later in conquered Savannah, when Sherman's perceived "generosity" was neither embraced nor lauded by those he had vanquished. With his proslavery sympathies, Sherman got along well with some of the residents of Memphis, telling them frankly how disappointed he was that the Northern abolitionists made an issue of the practice. In Memphis he also sought to relax martial law and to restore his version of law and order. He managed to handle some issues deftly. Many blacks had fled their bondage and streamed into Memphis. He assigned about fifteen hundred of them to construction projects at Fort Pickering, where they were fed and clothed but not paid their wages until their legal status as freemen could be established. He expressed regret that he was unable to find employment for the women and children who accompanied many of these male workers. Sherman also relaxed the elaborate system of passes needed for white males to enter or leave the city, just as he repealed the prohibition on the service of all alcoholic beverages. When the city's leaders came to him expressing their wish to levy what we call today "sin taxes," Sherman permitted the majority of the taxes, exempting only the levies on the ownership of dogs and on the keeping of bordellos. As a former banker, Sherman proved himself probusiness while in charge of Memphis, although he and Grant were rebuked by higher authorities in Washington for trying to ban Jewish purchasing agents from exchanging cash for cotton.

Both generals feared that the South would immediately convert such cash to weapons and armaments. Sherman expressed this in anti-Semitic terms, stating that the "dishonest Jews" would smuggle ammunition and weapons into the South, barter them for bales of cotton, which they would then resell to the Northern mills. Grant also disparaged "Jewish speculators" on these same grounds. Sherman went so far as to propose a plan under which all money used in the purchase of cotton would be held by the federal government in escrow until the war was over, whereupon the vendors could apply for their withheld funds. The diplomatic and political consequences of a ban on the sale of cotton could have backfired hard on the interests of the Union. Neither general fully understood the implications of their proposition or how badly cotton was needed by the North for uniforms and tents for its troops and how wonderfully such a ban on the sale of cotton would have played into the hands of foreign nations interested in buying it, especially England for its Midland mills. Such a ban might have brought England into the war on the Confederate side, which was a distinct possibility for some time in the earlier part of the war. This is an example of how ill-suited military officers can be to politics, because their thinking is so often linear and one-dimensional.

Sherman again experienced the gracious social life of the South. After seeing to it that the theaters reopened, he often attended shows as he had done avidly for years. He formed friendships with judges and prelates in Memphis. He even attended church, which would have pleased Ellen enormously had the church only been Catholic and not Episcopal. The Episcopal bishop of Tennessee became a friend of his. In his biography *Sherman: A Soldier's Life*, author Lee Kennett reported yet another notable feature of this Memphis sojourn. Sherman formed a close friendship with Felicia Shover, the widow of an officer he had previously served with. So familiar in tone are Sherman's letters to her that biographer Kennett, alleging nothing more, believes these letters would not have made pleasant reading for Ellen. As usual, Sherman took umbrage at the Northern press after stories ran that he had become too cozy with the people who had run Memphis before the Union invasion. The Northern press claimed that Sherman had compromised Northern interests by enabling the same local Confederate ruling class to retain power. Such negative coverage in the North of Sherman's Memphis administration only increased his disdain for the press.

Although he did an acceptable job of governing Memphis, Sherman, an absolutist, overstepped his boundaries. He interfered with the administration of the civil and criminal courts in a high-handed fashion, claiming that under the "rules of war" his court-martial took precedence over civil authority. This presumption caused Sherman more than once to be overruled by higher command. In one instance, where Sherman's sentence for an alleged miscreant was especially draconian, even Grant had to intervene and countermand him.

As blind and unsympathetic to others as Sherman could often be, he left his post in Memphis in the spring of 1863 with the firm conviction that he was beloved by the city. This was far from the truth, but it proved not to matter. Halleck repaired to Washington to assume his new post as general in chief and left Grant now in charge of the war in the West; and Grant wanted Sherman alongside for the siege of Vicksburg.

Strategically, Vicksburg was the most important prize yet targeted by the Union. A Southern stronghold on the eastern bank of the Mississippi, the town played host to a fearsome fort that sat high atop rolling hills, its access impeded by steep bluffs. Heavily fortified by the Confederacy, the fort boasted many well-placed cannons that controlled all river traffic on the Mississippi. Ever since the outbreak of hostilities, the artillery at Vicksburg had sunk untold numbers of Union ships, including gunboats with which it had exchanged heavy fire. As a result, the Confederacy dominated the Mississippi River from Vicksburg all the way down to the river's terminus at the Gulf of Mexico, below New Orleans. Thus, the Trans-Mississippian states of the Confederacy were not divided from the main states lying east of the mighty river, and supplies and personnel could easily travel from the western reaches of the Confederacy in Texas through its eastern mainland and on to its Atlantic seaboard.

With the Confederate railroad lines still intact on either side of the river, transportation on an east-west axis straight across the Deep South states was functioning smoothly. President Lincoln, Secretary of War Stanton, and General in Chief Halleck, however, wanted this arrangement disrupted. Grant was called upon as commander of the Army of Tennessee to capture Vicksburg, a difficult and tricky assignment. Sherman was only too ready to accommodate his esteemed friend's order. He welcomed a return to the field after overseeing civilian commerce in Memphis for nearly half a year. But when Grant first contacted Sherman at the end of November 1862 about the Vicksburg mission, Sherman had no idea how physically taxing and psychologically stressful his subordinate role would be. In fact, Grant would launch two highly costly attacks before being able, finally, to secure the fort and the town for the Union. In all three efforts, Sherman and his troops shouldered heavy responsibilities, suffering many hardships.

The entire campaign for Vicksburg stretched from late November 1862 to July 4, 1863. So unendurable were the conditions imposed on the town during that long stretch—the final strangling siege lasted from early May to July 4—that the national holiday of Independence Day would not be celebrated in Vicksburg until World War II. Toward the end of the siege, hardly any life could be found within city limits. The townspeople had abandoned their homes in favor of caves dug into the hillside (the better to survive the constant Union bombardment), while stragglers in town were suffering mightily from dysentery, diarrhea, malnutrition, camp fever, typhoid, unsanitary conditions, and other nearly unbearable deprivations. Grant's initial orders to Sherman had him gathering his troops at Memphis and, using a hastily assembled flotilla, heading south on the Mississippi to the mouth of the Yazoo, a few miles north of Vicksburg. A friend Sherman had recently made, Rear Admiral David Dixon Porter, aided in this maneuver. Porter reconnoitered the Yazoo and determined that it was infected with primitive torpedo floats, an early form of the submerged mine. Indeed, one of them had blown Porter's ironclad *Cairo* to bits.

Sherman's flotilla had to wait until waterborne engineers removed these potentially lethal mechanisms. When the engineers finished, Sherman headed up the river with his troops, only to meet with defeat when he engaged the Confederates at Chickasaw Bayou. Meanwhile, Grant had marched his troops to the east of Vicksburg, intending to assail the town and its fort on all three of its landlocked sides. He had ordered another subordinate, General Nathaniel P. Banks, to attack with his troops from the south. This plan fell apart when Grant's vital supply depot at Holly Springs, Mississippi, was attacked and burned to the ground by the able Confederate cavalry. Banks, too, like Sherman and Grant, encountered obstacles and was late in arriving on the scene. This combination of setbacks put an end to Grant's strategy to swiftly overtake Vicksburg by putting it between "the hammer and the anvil." Nevertheless, he took the setback in stride and planned his next attack.

The second attack entailed Grant moving past the Vicksburg guns at the bend in the river, although this maneuver entailed great peril for the ships and the men on them. With the help of Admiral Porter, Grant managed to pull this bold plan off by having the ships move under cover of night, escorted by Porter's gunboats. All of the Union ships with one exception made it by the big guns unscathed, despite the wise Confederate tactic of torching houses along the bluffs to illuminate the enemy. Charles

A. Dana, the celebrated journalist then serving as assistant secretary of war, counted 525 rounds fired at the Union ships out on the river that night.

After enduring this Confederate display of what might be dubbed an early instance of shock and awe, Grant and his army attacked overland from the south, which at first did not go well. There were too many logistical problems with the terrain. Canals had to be dug and other feats executed before Grant could mount a proper attack. Indeed, Grant was in a precarious position. With his army positioned well south of Vicksburg on the eastern bank of the Mississippi, he realized that he and his army might well be placed between the hammer and the anvil themselves. Confederate general Joseph E. Johnston (no relation to Albert Sidney Johnston) was gathering troops to possibly drive toward Grant from the east. With the fort looming to the north and the mighty river to the west, Grant would be hemmed in on three sides, since Banks had still failed to show up. If this maneuver succeeded, Johnston could drive Grant west into the river. What's more, Grant had stretched the distance too far between his army and his resupply depot back at Milliken's Bend. Just as the Confederate cavalry had burned his depot at Holly Springs, they might easily now sever his sole line of supply.

After contemplating this bleak scenario, Grant devised a brilliant strategy: escape this vulnerable bind by marching immediately, despite the risk of lacking a reliable and secure supply line. Because it was early spring and he and his army were surrounded by lush farmland, Grant correctly figured that his troops could forage and live off the land to an adequate degree, supplementing their rations with commandeered produce and livestock. The army actually thrived better on this improvised diet than it had on army rations alone. Sherman was promptly ordered to bring 120 wagons loaded with rations. He joined forces with Grant and marched east to defuse the gathering threat from General Johnston. Grant and Sherman took the state capital of Jackson, successfully driving off Johnston and his army.

Grant then backtracked, moving his army west, and defeated the commander of Vicksburg, Confederate general John C. Pemberton, at Champion Hill. Finally, Grant surrounded Vicksburg and commenced to subject the town and its fort to the brutal artillery siege that led to its Independence Day surrender. The "Gibraltar of Dixie" at last fell to Grant. Washington was overjoyed at news of this victory. The previous day, July 3, General Meade had repulsed the Confederate army under Lee at Gettysburg, the farthest penetration of the North by the South during the entire war. The Union now had a major advantage, and nobody could take more credit than Grant and Sherman. Already a national hero, Grant saw his star rise higher and took Sherman along with him for the glory ride, lauding him in his official report for his able assistance in the triumphant Vicksburg Campaign. This praise and recognition cheered Sherman, who had long been brooding for a number of reasons. His devastating defeat at Chickasaw Bayou weighed on his mind as a humiliating military failure. Sherman's patience had further been strained by clashes with the press's harsh criticism of the debacle. He was especially enraged with Thomas Knox, a reporter with the *New York Herald*. Knox had impersonated a soldier to get an inside story about Sherman, and Sherman wanted him executed for espionage. Sherman's anger was apparently fueled by frustration over his failure to suppress negative press coverage of his performance.

And Sherman was upset that earlier in the campaign he had been subordinated briefly to General John A. McClernand. Detested by Grant and Sherman, McClernand was a Lincoln favorite from their mutual home state of Illinois. The two weathered generals saw only an unqualified and overly ambitious amateur graced by favoritism. Perhaps some aspect of this formula resonated with Sherman's self-worth, pricking his fragile pride.

Despite causing his wife serious worry in his negative letters to her over these setbacks, Sherman held himself together throughout the Vicksburg Campaign and came through it very well. Thanks to Grant, he emerged with plaudits and with a promotion to brigadier general in the regular, as opposed to the volunteer, army. Privately, however, Sherman blamed Grant for the debacle at Chickasaw Bayou, ascribing his defeat to Grant's inferior planning and strategy. Again privately, Sherman vented at Lincoln, his career savior, for placing the detested McClernand over him. All of this would melt into the background soon, however, in light of devastating personal tragedy.

Sherman and his exhausted troops declined to pursue the fleeing Johnston after ousting him from Jackson and instead returned to Vicksburg and bivouacked along the Black River. Several weeks of relaxation and recovery ensued. Not only had Sherman been promoted to brigadier general in the regular army, he had also received congratulations from important officials in Washington, including a glowing letter from General in Chief

Halleck. Sherman extended invitations, welcoming visitors to his encampment. Ellen made the trip to Mississippi, bringing along the four oldest children. Their father set them up in tents and allowed them to explore the camp and mingle among his troops. His oldest and favorite son Willy accompanied him to drills and exercises and was even named an honorary regimental sergeant. Things were fairly idyllic for the family and the troops, who were relishing their recuperation time. After a few peaceful weeks, Sherman received word from Grant that General William Rosecrans's Army of the Cumberland was pinned down to the east at Chattanooga. On September 19 and 20, they had taken a thrashing at the Battle of Chickamauga from the Confederate Army of Tennessee, under the command of Sherman's old friend Braxton Bragg. Rosecrans now faced the twin options of surrender or starvation. Determined and decisive as ever, Grant immediately prepared for their rescue, instructing Sherman to mobilize his troops and proceed rapidly to Chattanooga.

Sherman hastily made arrangements to ship his family back to Lancaster. While loading onto the ship for the trip upriver, Sherman and Ellen noticed that Willy was pallid and sick. An army physician was quickly summoned. Dr. E. O. F. Roler, of the Fifty-fifth Illinois, suspected camp dysentery and typhoid fever. He instructed the family to get Willy to Memphis immediately, where better care was available. The Shermans reached Memphis with all due haste and installed Willy in the Gayoso Hotel, the site of Sherman's former headquarters as military governor of the city. Shortly thereafter, the family was informed that the situation was dire. On October 3, in the late afternoon, Willy died. Sherman sank into his own private hell, rocked by this catastrophic loss. Naturally, his performance suffered. Instead of hastily executing Grant's order, Sherman mired himself in micromanaging details, such as arranging overly elaborate rail transport for his troops and focusing on transporting an unnecessarily large number of supply and ration wagons. Grant was patient and forgiving toward this behavior, despite criticism from his fellow generals, many of whom held Sherman in low regard. His peers viewed Sherman the same way Sherman viewed McClernand—as overrated and privileged, largely indebted to his family for his career advancement.

Finally Grant cracked down, demanding that Sherman get moving, depressed or not. He was ordered to forget about advancing all the supply wagons and instead to march the troops around them and proceed immediately to their new battle lines. The pressure was on. The Confederates had moved another army south from Virginia into Tennessee under General James Longstreet, threatening to encircle General Ambrose Burnside at Knoxville. If this maneuvering by the Confederates was not thwarted immediately, the number of troops at their disposal for battle would be equal to that of the Federals. Sherman and his army had to arrive in time to help relieve Rosecrans at Chattanooga, or risk a massive confrontation between armies of equal strength, should Longstreet overwhelm Burnside and move southwest to join the battle at Chattanooga. Grant wanted to forestall this possibility.

Sherman and his army arrived in time at the hilly site of the battle for Chattanooga, Missionary Ridge, though they arrived much later than they could have. Sherman, commissioned to engage battle with an old dear friend, was given the all-important assignment to attack Bragg's right flank and thereby spearhead the Union attack. Instead of moving swiftly to accomplish this crucial objective, Sherman hesitated. His hesitation allowed Bragg to shift troops to his right flank, reinforcing it. The result was a bloody standoff, but with the luck that seemed to favor Sherman so often, Union forces attacking under Generals Joseph Hooker and George Thomas accomplished the breakthrough, principally on the Confederate left flank. Hooker took the superlative natural redoubt of Lookout Mountain while Thomas pushed Bragg's troops back in the center of the line. Grant, observing Sherman's failure to breach and roll up Bragg's right flank, ordered Thomas to attack straight ahead. So concerned had Grant become with the execution of his strategy at Chattanooga in a fashion timely enough to intercept General Longstreet's arrival from Knoxville, he hastened to Missionary Ridge and took personal command alongside General Thomas in the center of the battle lines. It was Bragg's right flank that controlled access to the principal rail line, Bragg's chief avenue of resupply. Bragg's right flank also controlled access to the key roads General Longstreet would need should he and his army arrive from Knoxville in time. By the time the Union succeeded in controlling these roads, it didn't matter much because Longstreet had chosen to stay in Knoxville, menacing Burnside.

Sherman was dispatched to Knoxville to relieve Burnside as soon as the victory at Missionary Ridge was secured. It's clear that Grant had reservations about Sherman's ability to carry out this Knoxville mission in a timely manner. Grant assigned his staff officer General James H. Wilson to accompany Sherman and report on his performance. Wilson was not impressed with

Sherman—indeed, he reported to Grant twice that Sherman was again dawdling, and that he had to prod him repeatedly to put on speed. At any rate, word arrived from Burnside that Longstreet had suddenly broken off his siege of Knoxville and withdrawn. The most likely explanation for Longstreet's withdrawal is that word of Bragg's withdrawal at Chattanooga had reached him. No doubt Longstreet believed that his own position was too vulnerable to the victorious Union forces moving up from Chattanooga, as indeed was the case. Once again, Sherman opted out of pursuing the fleeing enemy, as his men were too exhausted from traveling hundreds of miles during the past two months. Footsore, hungry, and overextended, they needed to rest and recoup their energy.

All things considered, 1863 was not a great year for Sherman. After the high-water mark of victory at Shiloh in April 1862, followed by the ego-boosting military governorship of Memphis to top it off, he had sustained a series of setbacks in the spring of 1863—especially the humiliating defeat at Chickasaw Bayou— that preceded the ultimate victory at Vicksburg in July. Then had followed the exhausting and fruitless high summer pursuit of the withdrawing Johnston and his Confederate Army of Tennessee deeper into Mississippi in heat so gruesome that Sherman's troops had to march at night. This exhausting assignment was succeeded too quickly in early autumn by the loss of his beloved Willy. Without any time to mourn, Sherman was forced into his abysmal performance in early winter at Chattanooga, followed by the futile march to Knoxville.

At year's end Sherman's mood was dark indeed. He was again brooding and depressed. He was most eager, consequently, to grab the kudos extended him by the ever-generous Grant, who truly went out of his way to preserve Sherman's image. Grant's report on the Battle of Missionary Ridge portrayed Sherman's performance as one of heroism and sacrifice in pulling the majority of Bragg's troops into the defense of his right flank, thus making possible Hooker's triumph to the south at Lookout Mountain and Thomas's breakthrough in the center. This breakthrough had resulted from Grant's alert order—in light of Sherman's failure to deliver on his assignment—to attack straight ahead. Grant's report was pure revisionism, pure generosity toward his friend. Instead, Grant might more accurately have written of Sherman's desultory ineptness. Though many of Grant's staff and adjutants criticized Sherman's performance, as did Sherman's colleagues at Missionary Ridge, Hooker and Thomas, Grant covered for his friend.

In contrast Sherman was privately critical of Grant's generalship. He spoke of his lack of polish, class, education, and knowledge of military history, theory, strategy, and tactics. Sherman wasn't entirely alone in these critiques, but Abraham Lincoln, a man possessed of superior wisdom, saw matters differently and Grant was promoted to general in chief. As a direct consequence, Grant's promotion furnished Sherman with his own promotion to succeed Grant as head of the Union forces in the West. This ranking, which many believed was scarcely deserved, furnished Sherman with the position to launch himself into history and enduring fame.

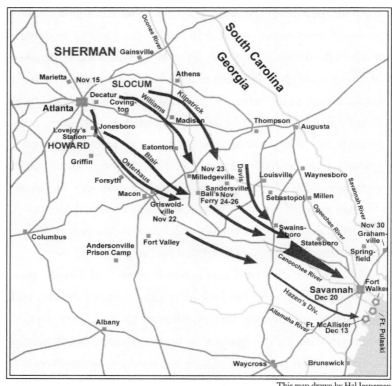

This map shows the path Sherman took in his March to the Sea.

TWELVE

Triumph and Tragedy

THE BEST YEAR of Sherman's life was upon him: 1864. At the beginning of the year, he led a marauding army into Mississippi in the Meridian Campaign, with the intention of wiping out any remaining ability of the Confederates to function in the state. Railroads and other strategically important facilities were the primary targets. Rails were torn up, heated in bonfires, and then twisted around the trunks of trees to form what became known as "Sherman neckties." By the time Sherman and his marauders returned north from Mississippi, the state was incapable of supporting a Confederate military presence there or anywhere in the adjacent Deep South states. As a result, none of these Deep South states could assemble an army to attack the Union armies clustered in and around Tennessee.

Often called simply the Army of the West, this one-hundred-thousand-man force comprised three separate armies: the Army of the Ohio, the Army of the Cumberland, and the Army of the Tennessee—Sherman's former command. With the Deep South neutered, Georgia, the largest state on the eastern seaboard and a key state in the Confederate war effort, was now exposed and vulnerable to attack. In March word came that Grant had been summoned to Washington to meet with the president. Since the start of the war, Lincoln had had a difficult time finding leaders he could trust with the war effort. First there had been the rout at First Bull Run under McDowell. That had been followed by Union setback after setback until finally McClellan won the great Union victory at Antietam in September 1862, only to forfeit its advantage by failing to pursue Lee. This failure on McClellan's part allowed Lee time to regroup his army and, like the great leader of men and the warrior he was, make a comeback and oversee the early 1863 trouncing of the Union's vaunted Army of the Potomac at Fredericksburg and Chancellorsville. The Union victory at Antietam, nevertheless, was monumental, keeping England and France from extending diplomatic recognition to the Confederacy.

Next came the midyear turnaround of 1863. On July 3 the Army of the Potomac under Meade repulsed Lee and his Army of Northern Virginia at Gettysburg. A day later, Grant delivered the great Union victory at Vicksburg. And in the intervening half year Grant followed up that victory with another at Chattanooga. Even after Lincoln had sent his friend the journalist Charles Dana, also the assistant secretary of war, to spy on Grant and evaluate his notorious drinking, by March Lincoln's mind was made up. Despite Grant's personal foibles, Lincoln put him in charge of the Union war effort. When Lincoln then promoted Grant to lieutenant general, he resurrected a rank not used since George Washington held it. Shortly before Grant's promotion, back at the end of December, Lincoln, Stanton, and Halleck had queried Grant about who should be appointed as commanding general of the Army of the Potomac, then opposing Lee in Virginia. Grant had recommended two generals: William Farrar "Baldy" Smith and Sherman. When pressed on which of the two candidates he favored, Grant, revealing doubts about his friend Sherman as a result of Sherman's sorry performance at Missionary Ridge, indicated that he preferred Smith. Later, Grant discovered that Lincoln, Stanton, and Halleck, too, had been against selecting Sherman. Then, three months later in March, everything changed. Lincoln summoned Grant to the capital, promoted him to general in chief in place of Halleck, and told Grant that it was up to him whether Meade continued as commanding general of the Army of the Potomac. Grant left Meade in place and then, loyal as ever, elevated Sherman to Grant's old post as commander of all Union forces in the West. Sherman, recently returned from his Meridian Campaign in Mississippi, was summoned to a meeting in Nashville with Grant and all the top generals in the Western Army. When the Nashville meeting ended, Grant started for Washington to assume his new duties, but told Sherman to accompany him to Cincinnati for a meeting first. Over the course of two days in a hotel room in Cincinnati's Burnet House, the two men pored over maps as Grant defined the strategy they would

use to win the war. Sherman later succinctly articulated this strategy: "He was to go for Lee, and I was to go for Joe Johnston."
Grant did not consider conquering territory as the objective of
the game. Rather, he determined to deflate the two principal
armies defending the Confederacy by pursuing them relentlessly
and engaging them in constant battle, simultaneously destroying
any strategic targets in their path. During the previous summer,
in Jackson, Mississippi, Grant had demonstrated to Sherman
exactly what he meant by "strategic targets," burning the rail system and the train depots, the supply warehouses, the smithies,
the machine shops, and the arsenals. In dispatching Sherman on
the recent Meridian Campaign, Grant had given him the same
mission. He was to disable and destroy the enemy's ability and
capacity to wage war.

The objective Grant now posited for the two-pronged attack
would be more of the same, only intensified. Grant explained that
Sherman and he would have to coordinate and press their dual
attacks with such ardor and constancy that Lee could not shift
troops and equipment to Joe Johnston, or vice versa. Though
separated by slightly more than five hundred miles, Lee and
Johnston must be kept under unstinting assault by the Union
armies. Though separated by the same distance, Grant and
Sherman must stay in constant contact to mutually ensure their
chances of success. As a result of this essential need for unbroken
communication, Sherman sent telegrams to Grant, sometimes as
many as several a day, until he undertook his famous March to the
Sea, when he operated while isolated and unable to communicate
with his superiors.

As Sherman readily acknowledged, under this new strategy Grant faced the bigger challenge. Lee was the most aggressive and successful general the South had, just as Grant was the most aggressive and successful the North had. Lee commanded the most experienced army of the Confederacy, as well as its largest, and Grant had the same two elements on his side. That spring, in the early days of May, hostilities commenced between these two great generals when Lee pressed Grant into battle at the Wilderness. Grant had moved the Army of the Potomac southward on what was called his Overland Campaign, with the Confederate capital of Richmond as the destination. Taking Richmond was not the object of the exercise. The objective was instead to shatter Lee's army along the way. The area of central Virginia—of which the Wilderness was a part—would witness the heaviest and most savage fighting of the entire war. From 1862 to 1864, when the Overland Campaign ended, this area of Virginia bore witness to one hundred thousand combatants killed on each side.

Grant tried to go around on Lee's right flank and place the Union army between Lee and Richmond. Lee, perceptive as ever, anticipated Grant's strategy and deftly countered by attacking head-on, precipitating the indescribably fierce Battle of the Wilderness. Accounts vary slightly, but Grant incurred roughly 17,500 casualties, while Lee incurred about 11,250. In a battle so costly and fierce, it is difficult to declare either side the victor. Grant was certainly thwarted, however, and his objective unrealized. Lee stymied Grant's advance and once again showed himself to be the quicker and more flexible pugilist.

If the pattern of previous commanders of the often-beaten

Army of the Potomac held true once again, the Union army would now fall back. But Grant was not just another Union commander. After Lee pulled his exhausted army back for a breather, Grant took a day for recuperation as well. When Grant issued orders to his subordinates the next day, they were instructed to turn toward Richmond once they cleared the woods and reached the road. Instead of withdrawing, Grant was going to press the attack. Grant moved his army farther to Lee's right flank, seeking for a second time to go around it and proceed toward Richmond.

Correctly reading Grant's intentions again, Lee countered by concentrating his army on his right flank. Within a week the even more intense Battle of Spotsylvania Court House erupted. Fighting there has since passed into legend, with the savage hand-to-hand combat at what was called "the Mule Shoe" lasting an uninterrupted twenty-three hours. Fought along a four-mile trench dug by Lee's army, this battle was even more costly than the Wilderness battle of the week before. Lee inflicted nearly 18,500 casualties on Grant while Grant inflicted nearly 13,500 in return. Grant and Lee both knew at this point that, due to outside reinforcements, Grant could sustain the losses and Lee could not. Grant recognized his advantage and exploited it over his opponent's two weaknesses—dwindling manpower and resources.

Before Grant launched his Overland Campaign, Lee and his army were outnumbered roughly two to one. Lee started with about sixty-two thousand men, and by the end of the Battle at Spotsylvania, he was down to just over fifty thousand. Grant, thanks to replacements and new recruits, still had twice that many. Grant's relentless war of attrition in Virginia would succeed, and his success there made possible Sherman's success in Tennessee, in Georgia, and in the Carolinas. For his heroic efforts Grant suffered stinging opprobrium in the Northern press. Lincoln ignored the calls for the "butcher's" (Grant's) replacement. Sherman, on the other hand, would be hailed in that same Northern press as a conquering hero, though the obstacles he confronted and the Confederate resistance he faced were far inferior to those surmounted by Grant.

While Grant struggled mightily in Virginia to overcome the South's best army, led by its best general, Sherman in Tennessee had to face the lesser challenge of overcoming General Joseph E. Johnston and the smaller and less experienced Confederate Army of Tennessee. A West Point classmate of Lee, Johnston was a master of deception and of wise and strategic retreating. Badly wounded earlier in the war during the Peninsula Campaign, Johnston was denigrated by his detractors as gun-shy. His proponents, however, saw him as a general who wisely recognized Sherman's overwhelmingly superior force of a hundred thousand men and attempted to jab at it, to wear it down.

With the determination and resilience he had absorbed from Grant, Sherman set about this task and pressed his attack hard. Along the route to Atlanta, Johnston set a perplexing pattern. As Sherman advanced against his dug-in army, attempting to flank it, Johnston would quickly foil the flanking movement by strategically retreating. At first there were slight preliminary skirmishes. Then Johnston offered brief resistance at both the Battle of Resaca and, shortly thereafter, at the Battle of Kennesaw Mountain, only to retreat again quickly from both encounters. This seemingly passive approach roiled the Confederate leaders in Richmond, especially President Jefferson Davis. Many historians believe this tactic was disastrous for the Confederacy. On July 17, Johnston was relieved of command and replaced by Lt. General John Bell Hood, even as Johnston was preparing his defenses for the Battle of Peachtree Creek.

Hood, too, had been seriously wounded in combat. At Gettysburg, his left arm sustained irreparable damage, rendering it almost completely useless. Then at Chickamauga he lost his right leg from the hip down. As a result of these wounds he was so severely incapacitated that it required four men to place him on his mount and strap him to it. He was a living symbol of the condition of the Confederacy. Once appointed to command the Army of Tennessee, Hood immediately engaged Sherman's army in three quick and costly battles, all losses for the Confederacy: Peachtree Creek on July 20, Atlanta on July 22, and Ezra Church on July 28.

The most important of these three battles was by far Atlanta, which actually took place in Decatur, a neighborhood to the east side of the city proper. Sherman was a bit standoffish in all three of these battles, allowing his subordinates more free reign than was custom. This decision may have cost him his best friend, Major General James B. "Mac" McPherson, a favorite of Grant as well, and the man who had succeeded Sherman as the commander of the Union Army of the Tennessee. On the afternoon of the Battle of Atlanta, Mac went forward to inspect the front lines, where a sniper fatally shot him. Sherman has been faulted for not reinforcing the attacking Army of the Tennessee under McPherson because he favored his old command above all others and wanted to see it take Atlanta unaided by either of the other two supporting armies under Sherman's command that day. At the end of the battle, it seemed evident that Hood had kept control of Atlanta, but just barely.

Six days later, the Confederates absorbed another defeat at Ezra Church. Sherman then decided, instead of engaging in any more subsidiary battles, to encircle the city and put it under siege. A constant bombardment ensued, lasting throughout the month of August. When Sherman managed to cut the rail line to Macon, Atlanta's only supply line, it was the final crippling blow. Hood pulled out of the city on September 2, after first burning the munitions in the Atlanta arsenals. The massive explosions could be heard for miles around by the encircling Union armies. Three days later, Sherman ordered the entire population of the city to be expelled. He had favored such deportations and forced migrations ever since his first posting as a second lieutenant in the Second Seminole War in Florida. Then, and after the Civil War, when the United States was handling Native Americans out West, Sherman was on written record in favor of forced expulsions, even extermination, and many officers accepted his views. Apparently these practices were not based on racial prejudice, as Sherman considered such treatment appropriate for the entire population of Atlanta as well, caring not at all that these residents were his fellow countrymen and countrywomen by his own inflexible unionist standards.

On September 7, Sherman moved into the city and set up his headquarters, where he stayed for the next two months. The conquest of Atlanta made banner headlines in the North and covered

Sherman in praise. It almost certainly contributed to Lincoln's reelection two months later, which in turn eliminated any possibility the Confederacy had to achieve a negotiated end to the war from Lincoln's opponent, General McClellan. In any event, during this two-month interval in Atlanta, Sherman was relentlessly severe in his repression of anyone he considered a rebel or a guerrilla. This included citizens who remained despite the evacuation of Atlanta and in turn might occupy territory operated in by Confederate cavalry. It also included any citizens suspected of being raiders, partisans, or saboteurs. Suspects were often summarily executed without any due process of law. Sherman had always favored extreme measures.

Earlier in his writings about the war, principally in letters to his brother John, Sherman had proposed that the entire South should be repopulated with settlers from Iowa and other western states, while the Southern troublemakers were off-loaded to Central and South American countries. There these displaced miscreants could pursue their former way of life, including retaining the ownership of their slaves, if they so desired.

By now Sherman's fame had spread. He was receiving fan mail as well as requests for his autograph or for locks of his hair. As he took sterner and more sweeping actions to punish anyone he deemed recalcitrant in the local population, Sherman engaged in negotiations to end the war. He undertook these negotiations without any authority to do so, perhaps acting out of an inflated ego. The Southern leaders he engaged in these talks—including the Unionists among them—were not fully cooperative, much to his surprise.

Soon Sherman had a new focus, a new campaign in the works. Since peace had not broken out as he deemed it should have in light of his supposedly magnanimous negotiations, he decided further hostilities were necessary. He set his cap on a march to the sea. He would conquer Savannah just as he had conquered Atlanta.

Before he left for Savannah, however, he famously ordered his troops to burn Atlanta to the ground. They left only about four hundred buildings standing. Historians vary in their estimates of how many buildings Sherman and his troops actually burned, ranging between three and five thousand. The majority of these decimated buildings had no bearing whatsoever on the South's capacity to wage further war. Combined with the torching of Atlanta, Sherman's Savannah Campaign, popularly known as Sherman's March to the Sea, doubly assured him the fame and celebrity he had sought for more than three decades. It secured his enduring recognition as a military innovator and genius by many military theorists and historians. Sherman never faced any significant opposition on the march. The novelty of the mission lay in the fact that he took an army of sixty thousand men 250 miles through Georgia in five weeks, without benefit of a secure supply line. Nor did he possess any means of communication.

Grant was Sherman's direct influence regarding such a strategy. At Vicksburg, Grant had demonstrated that an advancing army could risk having an insecure supply line by living off the land. Sherman tested Grant's accomplishment for himself in the Meridian Campaign, and again in his march on Atlanta, with an insecure supply line stretching back a hundred miles to

Chattanooga. In each of these three preliminary instances, however, the supply line was not more than a hundred miles away,
and Sherman intended to return to his point of origin fairly
soon. With his Savannah Campaign, however, Sherman was
going to march more than double this distance, while completely
incommunicado.

Sherman relied heavily on his superior memory in preparation for this march. During his time stationed at Charleston as
a young officer, he was dispatched to Georgia on army business
and covered on horseback the same terrain that his army would
now march through. As a result, he now knew in advance what
type of country they would be passing through. His memory was
phenomenal, but moreover his gifts as an accomplished artist had
sharpened his eye as an analyst of terrain, as had his work as a
surveyor. To augment all of these advantages, Sherman requisitioned the Federal government for the most recent census data
on the Georgia counties his army would pass through. This data
allowed him to gauge the amount of food, livestock, and crops
his army could forage. The tonnage of foodstuffs required to
feed an army of sixty thousand men was staggering. If the enemy
pinned Sherman and his army down for any extended period of
time, their strictly limited supplies and rations would quickly run
out, leaving only the prospects of surrender or starvation. Their
supply of rations was good only for twenty days, slightly more
than half the time it actually took them to reach Savannah.

The impetuous Hood had made Sherman's strategy easy to
accomplish. After withdrawing from Atlanta to Alabama, Hood
tried to draw Sherman's army to Tennessee by attacking its line

of supply between Chattanooga and Atlanta. Hood's gambit backfired. Sherman reacted wisely, splitting his huge army in two. Sixty thousand men marched on to Savannah, while the remaining forty thousand pursued Hood into Tennessee. Hood failed to sever Sherman's supply line, and he went on to engage the Union Army of the Ohio in Tennessee, losing to General John M. Schofield at the Battle of Franklin on November 30. Finally, on December 15 and 16 at the Battle of Nashville, he foolishly attacked and lost to the same army that by now was combined with the Army of the Cumberland under General Thomas.

Hood was relieved of command over what little was left of the Confederate Army of Tennessee. Hood's original strategy had been planned by Confederate president Jefferson Davis directly after Hood's withdrawal from Atlanta. The overall intent was to win in Tennessee and then to reinforce Lee in Petersburg, Virginia. But because Hood's disastrous schemes of attack never produced a victory in Tennessee, this strategy never came close to meeting its objective. Brave, impetuous, and foolish, Hood had not come by his nickname "Wooden Head" by accident. His replacement of General Johnston and the consequential abandonment of Atlanta are considered by many Southerners to have signified the loss of all hope for the Confederacy's future existence as a separate nation. Not only did Hood fail in drawing Sherman after him into Tennessee, he foolishly left the route Sherman would take to Savannah undefended, which turned out to be one of the great military blunders in American history.

For his March to the Sea Sherman organized his forces into two parallel columns. He assigned the Army of the Tennessee, now under Major General Oliver O. Howard, to proceed in a column on his right wing. The Army of Georgia formed the left wing, commanded by Major General Henry W. Slocum. These parallel columns would advance separated by a distance that varied slightly depending upon the terrain, generally no less than three and no more than ten miles apart. On their periphery, General Judson Kilpatrick would patrol and protect them with his cavalry. Sherman was not overly impressed with Kilpatrick, who was an amateur thespian and compulsive womanizer. An often-reckless combatant, Kilpatrick had acquired the nickname "Kilcavalry," so high was the mortality rate of his men.

Throughout the march, Sherman's army was harassed from time to time by Confederate general "Fighting Joe" Wheeler, the daring and pugnacious leader who liked to refer to himself as "the war child" since he was only in his twenties. There was also light and sporadic resistance offered by Lt. General William J. Hardee's troops, an understaffed and underequipped army designated officially by the Confederacy as the Department of South Carolina, Georgia, and Florida. Sherman marched his army so deceptively that he kept these forces completely off balance.

He sent one of his wings west toward Macon, and the other wing east toward Augusta. When the Confederates reacted and moved in front of these two towns, Sherman marched the majority of his army straight down the middle, avoiding all conflict. His men correctly saw this as a means for sparing their lives and increased their allegiance to Sherman for avoiding wasteful and unnecessary battles. Aware of Baron Jomini's emphasis on *celerite*, Sherman drove his army to move fast and avoid engaging the enemy if possible, thereby diminishing both regrettable casualties and avoidable delays. During the march Sherman exhorted his troops to cover between ten and fifteen miles a day. By this time they had taken to calling him affectionately "Uncle Billy." This nickname at first struck the elitist Sherman as disrespectful, but with time he came to embrace it. He dressed informally, as was his custom, and was often quite disheveled. This quality endeared him further to his troops, as did his habit of riding alongside and talking to them, visiting at night by their campfires, and inspecting them on their pickets.

With few exceptions, the army rolled along and made incredibly good time. The First Alabama Cavalry Regiment, a force composed entirely of Southern Unionists, formed Sherman's personal escort throughout the march. At Griswoldville, a small town outside Macon, the Federals came under attack from three brigades of Georgia militia. These brave but foolhardy Georgians assaulted a seasoned unit from Indiana, who brutally cut them down. Many of these untrained militiamen were middle-aged fathers and uncles who died alongside their teenaged sons and nephews. The militia had only single-shot musket rifles while the Federals had Spencer repeating rifles. The dug-in Federals could get off seven shots from their magazines to each single shot the charging militiamen could fire. What Sherman called "hard war" and what history would call "total war" was well under way. It carried along with it great cruelty, exemplified by the suffering at Griswoldville. This cruelty was true of both sides: in the case of Union foragers, called "bummers," the Confederate cavalry shot or hanged them summarily, sometimes simply slitting their throats. The Federals burned houses, barns, cotton gins and storage bins, train stations and depots, manufacturers, blacksmith shops, machine shops, arsenals, excess crops, and even entire towns if there was any suspicion that the residents were aiding the enemy. The total extent of this decimation was specified by Sherman's famous field order #120. When Sherman discovered that the Confederates had planted "torpedoes"—primitive land mines—along the roads that his troops would travel, he forced Confederate prisoners of war to test the ground ahead of his troops or to dig these torpedoes up and dispose of them. Sherman also loaded wagons with prisoners of war and rolled them over roads suspected of concealing the mines.

Sherman's March to the Sea, "hard war" in full effect, impacted civilians in staggeringly harsh ways. His unruly troops paid no attention to the guidelines Sherman had laid out in field order #120, which went so far as to counsel them against the use of bad language while foraging or commandeering livestock. An entire harvest was stolen and untold numbers of animals were killed or commandeered. Many of Sherman's men plundered freely and instances of rape were not uncommon. It's highly doubtful that exemplary language was employed at all times by Sherman's men engaged in these activities.

The Federal troops turned meaner whenever they incurred losses from the Confederate units harassing them. Retaliation was especially intense after the Union troops came upon the Confederate POW camp at Fort Lawton, outside the town of Millen. The barbaric living conditions of the half-starved and half-dead Union troops, who had been hastily evacuated to Savannah, so enraged the Federals that they promptly burned the entire town of Millen to the ground. Along the march, Union general Jefferson T. Davis, a Unionist Southerner with the same name as the Confederate president, destroyed a makeshift pontoon bridge behind him and his troops at Ebenezer Creek, thereby stranding on the far bank the large contingent of slaves following them. Wheeler's Confederate cavalry shadowing Davis's column was sure to capture and return these slaves to their owners. Now doubly desperate for freedom, many of these stranded slaves jumped into the deep and wide creek and attempted to swim across it whether they knew how or not. Risking death rather than return to a life of slavery, most of them drowned. When asked later about this treacherous act on Davis's part, Sherman defended it for military purposes, saying the slaves were a drag on Davis's progress and would only have formed a logistical hardship and a tactical hindrance had they continued in the train of his marching column. Davis, he said, had done the right thing.

Sherman famously remarked that "War is hell" and "War is cruel" and declared that one might just as well rage against the intensity of a thunderstorm as against the harsh realities of war, for all the good it would do. The theme of war's bestial nature was one of Sherman's favorites.

For their part, Sherman's army marched mostly unimpeded except for the occasional skirmish, usually confined to the periphery and totally ineffective in stopping their advance. For the last two weeks of the march, the rich opportunities for foraging evaporated once the marshes of the lowlands were reached. Here the only crop was rice, and Sherman's troops ate it three times a day, not an appealing diet. If they did not succeed in reaching the sea to be resupplied by Union ships, these troops would face the serious jeopardy of becoming famished and undernourished. Sherman's men reached the outskirts of Savannah on December 10 to find that Hardee had fortified the town by building earthworks and entrenching his men behind them. Hardee had also flooded the surrounding rice fields in the marshes, hoping to cause Sherman's men even more difficulty in finding provisions.

With Hardee's men placed between Sherman's forces and the Union navy, Sherman immediately shifted his cavalry south to Fort McAllister, situated a few miles below the city at the mouth of the Ogeechee River. By overwhelming this fort Sherman could more easily gain access to the Union navy ships waiting off the coast to resupply his troops. On December 13, he oversaw the attack from the roof of a nearby rice mill. The Federals succeeded within fifteen minutes marked by lethal hand-to-hand fighting, with combatants on both sides often incurring death by bayonet, side arm, or hunting knife. A good many Union casualties resulted from torpedoes buried in the ground in front of the earthworks. Now able to access Union navy vessels, Sherman resupplied his troops and off-loaded the necessary artillery to topple Savannah.

Four days later, on December 17, he sent Hardee an ultimatum, warning that he would not hesitate to flatten the most beautiful city in North America if Hardee did not peaceably surrender to him, surely a drastic and unnecessary move at this juncture in the war. Instead, Hardee fled that night, leading his men stealthily across the Savannah River on a pontoon bridge improvised from rice flats. The following morning the mayor, R.

D. Arnold, surrendered the city after securing a promise that its citizens and their property would go unharmed. Sherman and his XX Corps under General John White Geary occupied the city that afternoon. Sherman set up headquarters in the Green Mansion at 14 West Macon Street on Madison Square in the heart of the city. This mansion, built between 1853 and 1861, is still there, a National Historic Landmark, now called the Green-Meldrim Mansion, after a subsequent owner. One of the finest examples of Gothic Revival architecture in the South, the mansion today is a parish house for historic St. John's Episcopal Church, which stands next door. Sherman then sent his famous telegram of conquest to Lincoln: "I beg to present you as a Christmas gift the City of Savannah, with one hundred and fifty heavy guns and plenty of ammunition, also about twenty-five thousand bales of cotton."

The bales of cotton belonged to the owner of the mansion, Charles Green, who had spent ninety-three thousand dollars to build his splendid house, an astounding sum for that era. Lincoln, much pleased, wrote back to Sherman the following day. During the march, Lincoln had made the famous comment that Grant and he knew which hole Sherman went down but not which one he would come up.

Almost immediately Sherman set about planning his Carolina Campaign. This campaign launched in January and by February 17 Sherman and his troops had conquered Columbia, South Carolina, having torched every home and barn in its path. Sherman's army once again marched basically unimpeded, with only minor cavalry skirmishes on the wings of his two marauding columns. That afternoon Sherman lay down for a nap, only to find shadows of flames dancing on the bedroom wall when he awoke. Columbia had been torched. Who did it is a controversy to this day. Many people claim that the Federals caused it, others that fleeing Confederate cavalrymen set the fires. Sherman stated that he never "shed a tear over it" either way, and that he found it satisfying to "punish the state that had served as the crucible of secession" or, as Sherman usually termed it, "treason." By March 8, the rapidly advancing Federals crossed the state line into North Carolina. Eleven days later, from March 19 through March 21, the Battle of Bentonville took place, the only real battle in North Carolina. It pitted Sherman's vastly larger and better-equipped army against the remnants of whichever defeated Confederate armies General Joseph E. Johnston was able to scrape together. Johnston amalgamated the remnants of his old command, the Confederate Army of Tennessee, with troops culled from lesser Confederate armies.

Sherman made short work of Johnston during these three days of combat. When Johnston withdrew, Sherman stormed on, and in April he captured Raleigh, his third conquered state capital since he left his base at Chattanooga seven months earlier. The endgame had been set in motion months ago. Sherman was now in position to drive north toward Richmond and crush Lee between the jaws of a vise: Grant's Army of the Potomac attacking from the north, Sherman's army advancing from the south. Realizing this, on March 3 Lee withdrew his heavily battered army from the siege of Petersburg. By this point Grant's army alone outnumbered the beleaguered Lee and his Army of Northern Virginia by nearly three to one. With Petersburg fallen,

Grant required only nine more days to conquer Richmond on April 3. Six days later, on Palm Sunday, April 9, at Appomattox Court House, Lee rode in on his great mount, the indomitable war-horse Traveller, to surrender his army to Grant. Five days later, on April 14, Sherman commenced surrender negotiations with Johnston at Bennett Place outside Durham. In Washington that evening at Ford's Theater, John Wilkes Booth assassinated Lincoln. It was Good Friday.

On April 26, Johnston concluded his surrender to Sherman of more than eighty-nine thousand Confederate troops, scattered across the ten remaining states of the Confederacy outside Virginia. The most regrettable, heartbreaking, and horrendous war in American history was at an end.

This 1868 engraving by Alexander Hay Ritchie depicts the brutal destruction that took place during Sherman's March to the Sea.

Artist James E. Taylor gave this 1888 painting titled "From Atlanta to the Sea" to Sherman. It shows General William Tecumseh Sherman's "Bummers" striking it rich on a Georgia Plantation, burning cotton bales and the Gin House, gathering livestock, foraging provisions, and creating havoc on their March to the Sea.

Courtesy of the Archives of the University of Notre Dame

Exterior view of General Ulysses S. Grant's, later General William Tecumseh Sherman's, house at 207 I Street Washington, D.C. The photo is believed to have been taken in the early 1900s.

Courtesy of the Archives of the University of Notre Dame

Exterior view of General William Tecumseh Sherman's house at 912 Garrison Avenue, St. Louis, Missouri. Photo taken by Dr. William G. Swekosky in 1907.

Aftermath and Legacy

SHERMAN'S LIFE AFTER the war was not uneventful, but the aftermath of the nation's most savage and brutal conflict resounded perpetually, and every event afterward was cast under its shadow. Sherman had a post in the West for several years, during which his treatment of Native Americans reflected his innate anger and racism. Working with his friend General Philip H. Sheridan, he was brutal toward them. Like other white supremacists, Sherman and Sheridan regarded efforts by civilian "Indian agents" to "tame," "educate," and "civilize" these native people as misguided and futile. After uprooting them, Sherman and Sheridan wanted instead to shut them out and quarantine them on reservations where they could not harm white settlers. Both generals viewed the Native American lifestyle of hunting and gathering as archaic and out of step with the future of America as envisioned under the dictates of manifest destiny. With his usual despotic absolutism, Sherman performed his duties without qualm.

When Sherman attained the position of general in chief, he was petulant with Grant for thwarting his intentions toward the Native Americans, as well as for other decisions contrary to his wishes when it came to how the army should be run, most notably how the army should be free of civilian influence. Then Sherman's response to being subordinated to the civilian secretary of war was to sulk in St. Louis and write his memoirs. At another point he withdrew to live in Europe for a year. When, under austerity measures that required cutting the federal budget, Sherman's salary as general in chief was reduced from nineteen thousand to thirteen thousand dollars a year, he was outraged. He saw a nation for whom he had risked life and limb now expressing ingratitude toward her saviors. It should be noted that this was at a time when a private in the army earned two hundred dollars a year.

In 1884, Sherman retired to a life spent basking in glory on the speaker's circuit and strolling about New York City in full dress uniform, enjoying recognition and adulation. He also commonly attended gatherings of old soldiers, where he was invariably introduced to the rousing strains and stirring lyrics of "Marching Through Georgia," the hit song composed to commemorate his March to the Sea. During these years he became known for compulsively kissing young women and for flirting and carrying on with them. By this time his wife had become more withdrawn and reclusive, fervent about her Catholic faith to the point of compulsion. Her husband completely ignored her religious fervency. In an era long before movie stars, rock stars, and sports celebrities, Sherman's fame was monumental, equaled only by famous authors such as Mark Twain and Rudyard Kipling. Sherman and Grant were considered the most instrumental men in saving the republic now that Lincoln was long dead. Grant, too, predeceased Sherman, when he died of cancer in 1885, shortly after completing his benchmark memoirs.

Sherman's fame spread to Europe within his lifetime. All of the major European powers had sent high-ranking military personnel to America to witness and learn from the Civil War, that initial, most innovative, most groundbreaking, and most precedent-setting of modern wars. Military practices pioneered in the Civil War were reprised in Europe, especially by the Prussians. They closely studied the strategy, tactics, logistics, techniques, equipment, and weapons used by the Americans. In the Franco-Prussian War, the Prussians made great tactical use of their extensive railroad system, a technique learned from the Civil War. They also mounted the sustained siege of Paris from afar using outsized artillery like Big Bertha, which was reminiscent of the use of artillery Grant employed—the long-range "Dictator"—in his siege of Petersburg. In World War I, the horrors of trench warfare were realized on a larger and even more lethal scale than had been pioneered by any Civil War generals. In British military theorist B. H. Liddell Hart's writings, published between World War I and II, trench warfare would be correctly criticized as a gross, wasteful, and pointless approach to waging war. Liddell Hart's study of great military leaders throughout history gave voice to the strategy of "indirect approach," with its emphasis on speed of attack, avoiding prolonged and unproductive sieges, costly set-piece standoffs, and bloody stalemates. All of these negative aspects specifically characterized trench warfare.

Liddell Hart played an important part in the inflation of Sherman's fame and legacy. When asked in 1928 to write a book on a great American Civil War general, "preferably Lee," Liddell Hart instead fastened on Sherman, characterizing him as "an original genius." For Liddell Hart, Sherman's March to the Sea illustrated the efficacy of rapid movement in modern warfare, highlighting above all else the supreme need for speed. Once again, this strategy had been emphasized in the writings of Baron Jomini a century earlier, in his analysis of Napoleon, who in turn had learned much of it from Frederick the Great of Prussia. At West Point, Sherman had absorbed the importance of speed in warfare from Jomini, as taught to him by Professor Dennis Hart Mahan. Sherman had learned well from his mentors. As tanks were first being used during World War I, Liddell Hart exalted Sherman in his biography as a role model for rapid armored-mobile warfare. At the advent of World War II, the German High Command, consisting of Generals Heinz Guderian and Erwin Rommel, both of whom had read Liddell Hart's writings, perfected the concept of rapid armored-mobile warfare and called it *Blitzkrieg*. They had both doubtless also studied an influential article on Sherman published in German in 1876 by Captain A. von Clausewitz. Von Clausewitz was a relative of the seminal military theorist Carl von Clausewitz, Baron Jomini's great rival in that field. Captain A. von Clausewitz based his influential article principally on a translation of the Atlanta chapter from Sherman's *Memoirs*.

Finally, Sherman's March to the Sea quite famously influenced an outstanding proponent of rapid armored-mobile warfare, the legendary American general George S. Patton Jr. Patton studied Sherman's March to the Sea, retracing its route on foot and by car, before World War II.

Sherman's March to the Sea influenced military strategy and tactics to a legendary degree—even Patton's tanks were famously named for Sherman.

That Sherman's legacy has continued to influence generations of military leaders is without question. Also without question is his legacy of immoral and vile destruction of civilian life and property. In remembering this troubling man, both his greater and his lesser nature must be kept in view. He was right in saying that "War is hell." Statesmen and military leaders should remember this phrase and take it as certainty that war is indeed an unleashing of the bloody, unrestrained passions of humanity. If statesmen heed this advice, then pondering the life of William Tecumseh Sherman will have borne fruit worthy of the labor, especially in light of Ernest Hemingway's bull's-eye observation that in modern wars there are no winners.

Bibliography

Catton, Bruce. *The American Heritage New History of the Civil War*. New York: Viking Penguin, 1996.

Davis, Burke. *The Civil War: Strange and Fascinating Facts*. New York: Wings Book, a division of Random House, 1996.

Flood, Charles Bracelen. *Grant and Sherman: The Friendship That Won The Civil War*. New York: Farrar, Straus and Giroux, 2005.

Hardin, David. *After the War: The Lives and Images of Major Civil War Figures After the Shooting Stopped*. Chicago: Ivan R. Dee, 2010.

Hirshson, Stanley P. *The White Tecumseh: A Biography of General William T. Sherman*. New York: John Wiley & Sons, 1997.

Kennett, Lee. *Sherman: A Soldier's Life*. New York: HarperCollins Publishers, 2001.

_____. *Marching Through Georgia: The Story of Soldiers and Civilians During Sherman's Campaign*. New York: HarperCollins Publishers, 1995.

Lewis, Lloyd. *Sherman: Fighting Prophet*. New York: Harcourt, Brace and Company, 1932.

Liddell Hart, B. H. *Great Captains Unveiled*. New York: Da Capo Press, 1996.

_____. *Sherman: Soldier, Realist, American*. New York: Da Capo Press, 1993.

_____. *Strategy*. New York: Da Capo Press, 1993.

Marszalek, John F. *Sherman: A Soldier's Passion for Order*. New York: The Free Press, 1993.

McPherson, James M. *Battle Cry of Freedom: The Civil War Era.* New York: Oxford University Press, 1988.

Sherman, William T. *The Memoirs of General W. T. Sherman.* Teddington, England: The Echo Library, 2006.

Simpson, Brooks D. and Berlin, Jean V. *Sherman's Civil War: Selected Correspondence of William T. Sherman, 1860-1865.* Chapel Hill: The University of North Carolina Press, 1999.

Ward, Geoffrey C., with Ric Burns and Ken Burns, *The Civil War.* New York: Knopf, 1990.

Weintraub, Stanley. *General Sherman's Christmas.* New York: HarperCollins Publishers, 2009.

Acknowledgments

WE THANK OUR agent, Alexander C. Hoyt, and our publisher, Joel Miller, without whose initiative and talents this biography would not have been possible. Our editor, the gifted and unfailingly gracious Stephen Mansfield, guided and edited us brilliantly every step of the way. For their vital support and research, we thank Alexander Merrow and Tomoko Otsuka. Lisa Pellegrino deserves kudos for researching and selecting the photographs and maps. Linda Jo Calloway, Ed Carpenter, and Hugh Van Dusen offered excellent editorial suggestions and commentary.

We are indebted heavily to the authors of the books listed in the bibliography, most especially to professors Hirshson, Kennett, Marszalek, McPherson, and Weintraub, as well as to Bruce Catton and Charles Bracelen Flood.

The following four individuals and their institutions were gracious and helpful with crucial primary research: Charles Lamb, Assistant Director, University of Notre Dame Archives; Ashley E. Berry, Supervisory Park Ranger, Shiloh National Military Park; Keith Bridge, Historical Map and Chart Collection Team, National Oceanic and Atmospheric Administration; and Barry Cowan, Assistant Archivist, University Archives, Hill Memorial Library, Louisiana State University.

For invaluable secondary source research we salute the peerless staff of the Heermance Memorial Library in Coxsackie, New York: Linda Doubert, Sandra Stephen, Lynn Erceg, Lorri Field, Christine Reda, and Jacqueline Whitbeck.

About the Authors

AGOSTINO VON HASSELL spent his formative years in the United States, studying European History at Columbia University, graduating with a B.A. in 1974. He then attended Columbia Journalism School, graduating with awards in 1975. He is the president of The Repton Group LLC. Hassell has extensive expertise in national security matters, high-level investigations around the globe, terrorism and military issues and global trade problems.

ED BRESLIN is a writer living in New York and in the Hudson River Valley

THE ‖ GENERALS ★

Series Editor **Stephen Mansfield**

A series about leaders who stood out above the rest. Each general is known for his character and his drive to constantly strive for more. Of course each one has his flaws, but their ability to lead others and the loyalty shown by their soldiers establish these generals as historical figures worthy of recognition and study.

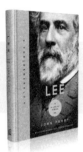

**Lee:
A Life of Virtue**
By John Perry

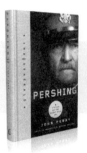

**Pershing:
Commander
of the Great War**
By John Perry

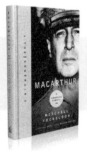

**MacArthur:
America's General**
By Mitchell Yockelson

**Sherman:
The Ruthless Victor**
By Agostino von Hassell
and Ed Breslin

**Patton:
The Pursuit of Destiny**
By Agostino von Hassell
and Ed Breslin

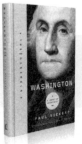

**Washington:
A Legacy of Leadership**
By Paul S. Vickery

Available wherever books and ebooks are sold.